Prophetic Evangelism Made Simple

Prophetic Evangelism Made Simple

Prophetic Seed Sowing

Matthew Robert Payne

Scripture taken from the New King James Version®. Copyright Scripture taken from the New King James Version®. Copyright© 1982 by Thomas Nelson. Used by permission. All rights reserved

ISBN-13: 978-1500439064
ISBN-10: 1500439061

You can contact Matthew via his website at http://www.matthewrobertpayneministies.net

Or join the Facebook Group that he admins called "Open Heavens and Intimacy with Jesus"

Acknowledgements

Jesus: I want to thank you, Jesus, for giving me the opportunity to witness to people in this manner. Thank you for leading me and giving me the things to say to people. You are forever my friend and your friendship is dear to me. You have blessed me with a good prophetic gift and without that gift, this book would not have been written.

My Mother, June: This book would not be in a great readable format if it were not for my mother, June. I want to thank her for the many hours that it took to edit this book. She made a real difference to what was first written and as it stands today.

Readers: Without knowing that there is one day going to be hundreds of readers who take my writings and advice out to the streets, this book would not have been written. I pray that you enjoy this book and put it into practice.

Dedications

Julia Achleitner

I want to thank Julia for being part of my life online. She has been good friend and she has enncouraged me many times with prophecies. Julia gives me a clear example of how loving I can be and how full of joy I can be in life. It is for Julia and people like her that this book is written. I would love her to know just how special she is to me.

Mark Stibbe

I wish to thank you, Mark, for better explaining Prophetic Evangelism with me through your book titled *"Prophetic Evangelism."* I hope that everyone who reads my book on the subject will also learn from what you have written. I have read your book three times now and I don't think I will ever tire of the stories you tell in it. You have done great things for the world of evangelism through your book and lectures.

Father, Son and Holy Spirit

I thank You, God, for Your beautiful ways and purposes in my life. I thank You first for giving me the gift of prophecy, then teaching me, through Mark Stibbe's book, what my gift actually was. I thank You for the thousands of messages You have given me and all the joy You have given me when I delivered them to others. I thank You for inspiring me to write another book on this vital subject for the people of God to read and be impacted by. I pray that You anoint this book and inspire people to respond to its teaching.

Forward

Matthew Payne's Prophetic Evangelism Made simple will draw you into the joyful adventure of partnering with God in evangelism. Matthew's passion for God and his heart for lost souls is unquestionable.

I have had the privilege of meeting and interacting with Matthew Robert Payne. He is the real deal. A true prophet of the Lord Jesus Christ with a heart of gold. Having received and witnessed his prophetic ministry, I can personally attest to its accuracy. Matthew is uniquely qualified to write this book, having had several thousand Prophetic Evangelism Encounters. This is the type of book I wish had been written when I embarked on a lifestyle of prophetic evangelism. Prophetic Evangelism Made Simple will take you by the hand and show you exactly what you need to be effective in using your prophetic gifts to reach people for the Lord.

I have written a book on Prophetic Evangelism and have trained and activated several persons in living a lifestyle of the miraculous and walking in the prophetic and prophetic evangelism over the past ten years and I wholeheartedly recommend anyone who is interested in Prophetic Evangelism to read this book and watch your life change as well as those all around you. There is a cry among the nations, "Who is God?" and "Does He care for me?". Through Prophetic Evangelism we get to speak the voice of God to those who don't know him yet and see their lives transformed.

This book is an encouragement to anybody who wants to live a supernatural lifestyle. Now Matthew's wealth of experience and keen insight is available to you..

Simon Peter
Author,
Prophetic Evangelism
Healing is Easy
Bringing Heaven to Earth
DayOfWonders.com

Table of Contents

one

The Great Commission

Before I begin this book, I'd like to start with a word of prayer.

"Dear Jesus, I pray that You will enlighten the readers of this book, so that they will plainly understand my words. I pray that You would not only enlighten them on what is going on and teach them what I mean, but also that Your Holy Spirit would light a fire within them to evangelize and to share your messages with people in the surrounding districts and the towns where they live.

I pray that you would illuminate Yourself in them and that Your compassion and love would start to enlarge their heart, so as to receive revelation and messages for the people around them. I pray that no matter how much fear may come against them from the Evil one, that they would step forth in love and minister Your grace to people they meet in their towns and wherever they go.

I pray that you'd encourage every reader to share this book with others and to share it on the Internet. I pray that this book would achieve everything that You have commissioned it to achieve. Thank You so very much for answering my prayer. I ask these things in Jesus' name. Amen."

I want to commence with a couple of stories that will undergird what I have to say in this book.

The first story happened thirty-one years ago when I was a lad of fourteen. I was sitting in my usual church and we had a visiting pastor come to share a message one night. He was preaching about being

Christ to our generation and in the middle of his sermon, he told a story which I will never forget. He said:

"I was in a shopping mall one day and was lifting my goods out of my trolley whilst in the checkout queue. It soon became obvious to me that the lady in front being served was becoming quite embarrassed at the register. Apparently, she had grossly overspent and was timidly asking the checkout lady to remove and deduct certain items.

In my opinion, the only problem with what she was doing, was that the goods she was handing back to be deducted, were essential items like soap, washing powder, and milk. I felt in my spirit that this should not continue because this shopper deserves to have these essential items.

I quietly said to the checkout lady, "Please don't put them back. Put them through on her order and I'll pay for the lot."

The register lady was noticeably surprised, but the shopper was actually appalled! She begged me not to do it. But I gently insisted and paid the bill. I then instructed the lady to go back into the shop and fill a whole shopping trolley full of goods that she desired.

It was very difficult to convince her of this, but eventually she left and came back with half a trolley full of goods. With a smile, I sent her back and she returned with three-quarters of a trolley full, so I sent her back for the third time. My generosity towards her had obviously prevented her from initially filling up her trolley. Eventually, she came back with a full trolley. I paid for all her goods and helped her load them into her car.

Then the pastor smiled at our congregation and quietly said: "Now, you're wondering what else I said to her - like, did I tell her that I was a pastor and that Jesus loves her and that His gift of salvation is free, just as the groceries and does she want to accept Jesus?"

Our congregation loved stories like this and someone called out: "Yes, we're waiting, did you say that?"

The Pastor replied, "I didn't say anything of the sort. In fact, I didn't even tell her I was a Christian, let alone a pastor. But in the shopping mall that day, I was Jesus Christ to her. I met her at her need and I went beyond the call of love. I even paid for an extra shopping trolley full of goods for her and blessed her totally. I reckon - I actually blessed her socks off that day!"

He said, "It's important for you to obey the Holy Spirit. Wherever you travel in this world, it's good for you to obey what the Holy Spirit is telling you to do. The Holy Spirit is pretty smart and He's very capable of bringing a person to salvation. Your job is: just to be Jesus to people and shine His light to those you meet. Allow the Holy Spirit to use you in whatever form that takes."

That story was impressed upon me so deep that it affected my entire life. That day, I learnt that all I needed to be - was Jesus to the generation and that's what I have proceeded to do ever since.

The minister went on to say that he believes that one day in the future, that lady will be having the Gospel explained to her by someone and the person will use an analogy possibly like this: "The Gospel is just as if you needed a whole lot of shopping and a stranger totally paid for all your needs. We are to graciously accept God's wonderful gift. He is freely offering it to us all."

Because of what happened to her in the supermarket that day, this particular lady will immediately identify with the Gospel message. She will have a personal testimony to share with others: she will be able to say that someone did that once for her and her eyes will fill with tears from the memory as she accepts Jesus into her life.

The Pastor concluded: "It's not always up to us to do the Holy Spirit's job in leading a person to Jesus. Our job is to simply obey the Holy Spirit's voice within us and to do whatever He wants."

That true story still impacts my everyday life!

Over the years, I have come to the conclusion that often, people are leading others in a sinner's prayer, simply because of religion. What I mean is that a believer may feel that they are less of a Christian if they don't lead a person to Christ. Many of those salvations are done on street corners and done under pressure by a zealous Christian. The majority of those "converts" don't continue to grow in faith, even if they did initially try to change their lifestyle. They eventually fall away as illustrated in the Parable of the Sower. When pressure comes upon their lives because of their decision for Christ, they openly return to their former lifestyle.

Therefore, it's vital that we understand that whenever we do Prophetic Evangelism and share the Gospel with people, we only do what the Holy Spirit tells us to do! We only deliver the message that we're called to give and we don't pressure a person into deciding for Christ when the Holy Spirit hasn't prompted us to do so.

That's the first story I want to undergird this book with. I pray that like me, you will understand that God has called every believer to personally "be Christ" in this world. The word *Christian* means "little Christ." We're to be *little Christs* in this world! We're just to shine His light and bring His encouragement and His words and to demonstrate His lifestyle to people we meet.

The second story I want to share with you is regarding a prophecy that I received.

I used to go to a church where they had prophetic words given every service. If you wanted to be personally ministered to in this way, you simply lined up for a prophecy. Several members of the congregation were gifted in prophecy and used to give prophetic words.

I once went to this couple who were delivering these words. The man said to me that he could see a picture of me as being a large vessel sailing down a long river like the River Nile in Egypt, and from time to time, I'm unloading cargo.

I unload the cargo and then sail on down the river.

He said, "You never return to the place that you unloaded the cargo, but the Lord wants you to know that you're unloading cargo into fertile ground. This "fertile ground" is like the grass at the edge of the River Nile. The Lord wants you to understand that you're always unloading a cargo into fertile ground."

The man then asked me if I understood and I said that I did. I had understood completely what the Lord was saying to me.

I had given literally thousands of prophetic words to strangers in the street, yet up till then, I had only met about five people for a second time, to receive confirmation of how my prophetic word manifested in their lives. This image of a boat delivering cargo, therefore, was an accurate image of me giving prophetic words and continuing with life without seeing the fruit of those words.

It had been upsetting to me that I wasn't meeting people the second time and hearing confirmation that the prophetic word had taken root and bore fruit in people's lives. As a person gifted in prophecy, I often long for confirmation that I've been correct and my prophecies are coming true. The Lord knew my heart and used that particular prophetic message, so as to encourage me that everything was all right.

The point that I really want you to hear is that when you're out and about and the Holy Spirit highlights a person, to whom you are to give a prophetic word to, that the receiver of the word actually represents "fertile" ground! That's the ground of the good soil in the Parable of the Sower – it's good soil! That means the receiver will be a person whom the Holy Spirit is one day going to bring to salvation!

This is the reason you're giving the message to the person: to encourage them and plant a seed that will develop and be harvested one day as a life saved. So that prophetic word, about the vessel sailing down the River Nile, really encouraged and impacted me. I truly believe that every time I give a prophetic word, I am giving words to people who are fertile to be harvested for God's Kingdom, one future day.

I therefore want my two stories to encourage you.

First: Be the light of Christ to people - a "little Christ" to them! Shine His light into all those you meet as you go about your normal activities in life.

Second: Whenever you give prophetic words to people, don't be overly concerned about leading them into repeating a sinner's prayer, when the Holy Spirit is not prompting you to do it. In fact, don't allow the devil to place any obligation whatsoever upon you! Rather, trust in the leading of the Holy Spirit and let Him alone guide you.

Although the subject of this book is Prophetic Evangelism, a more appropriate title would be *Prophetic Seed Sowing*. This is what the Holy Spirit is actually doing in the lives of people. It is important that you understand that the Holy Spirit will illuminate people to you. He will show you the people to give a prophetic word to. These are people whom God is already working in.

In this first chapter, I want to encourage you not to worry. In fact, I will emphasize this: **do not worry!**

The Holy Spirit has your ministry totally under control and He knows what He's doing. He loves you and He's going to use you in the ministry of leading people to Him, leading them closer to Him, and eventually, leading them into salvation.

These two stories of mine are actually an introduction to what I say now. Jesus said in the end of the Gospel of Matthew, Chapter 28:18, *"All authority has been given to me in heaven and on earth. Go therefore, and make disciples of all the nations, baptizing them in the name of the Father, and of the Son, and of the Holy Spirit, teaching them to observe all things that I have commanded you: and lo, I am with you always, even to the end of the age. Amen."*

I realize that many Christians haven't led a person to Christ because they don't feel adequate to do so. This book is all about equipping a believer with tools that will assist them to lead others closer to Jesus Christ. Many Christians see the verse above and they feel guilty about it.

I want you to be encouraged that if you start to manifest a Christ-like life, Jesus will hold your hand and will be with you to the end of the age. He's going to be with you until He comes back in the sky. Therefore, you can be sure that when He says He'll be with you, that He will also be with you as you minister in Prophetic Evangelism. He will be standing right next to you as you deliver your prophetic words. You need not be afraid! Just be encouraged and know in your heart *that He will be inspiring your words!*

Again, please do not feel any obligation to have someone recite a sinner's prayer. Remember, it has always been the Holy Spirit's job to save anyone. It is actually impossible for a mere human to save anybody!

two

What Part Can I Play?

What part can you play in the Great Commission? What exactly are your duties in the Great Commission? How can you assist in leading a person to Jesus Christ?

One of the simplest ways to lead people to Jesus Christ or to bring Him into focus in a person's life is to just BE Jesus Christ to them! When they're angry - you should be easy going. When they're needy - you could perhaps supply their need. When they're frustrated - you should be the voice of calm. When they're lacking money, you could perhaps give it to them. Wherever possible, you could actually help someway in their need.

One time, after a full day of constant ministry, Jesus told His disciples that they would take their boat and cross over to the other side of the water. Once the men settled in the boat, Jesus took the opportunity to rest, so He made Himself comfortable on the floor of the boat and went to sleep. However, within a very short time, a raging storm developed which caused the terrified men to fear for their lives: these seasoned sailors feared their boat was going to sink!

The storm was abnormal: it was totally beyond their scope of experience! Never had they faced such terror! They knew beyond doubt that they could not battle their way through it and they were convinced that they were facing death! Even though they were furiously bailing out water, the boat was constantly filling up at an alarming rate. They simply couldn't bail out the water fast enough! Angrily, they woke up Jesus and accused him, saying "Don't you care that we die?"

Jesus briefly glanced at their terrified expressions and then He quietly stood up in the boat. He confronted the wind, the waves and the storm and commanded them to be at peace. Immediately, the storm settled! The disciples were greatly relieved, but they were totally awed by this miracle: the elements, part of creation itself, had bowed down to their Master's command!

Some preachers believe that the whole storm episode could have been a test for the disciples. I tend to agree. You see, these men had just spent an amazing day with their Master! They had even played a part in His awesome miracle of providing lunch for a tremendous crowd. On top of that, they had heard His parables and His teaching all day long!

Yet, in this crisis situation, they had forgotten all those things and had severely panicked, even when this same Jesus was IN the boat with them! Sheer terror had wiped their memory completely. Their faith had totally deserted them. They had forgotten what Jesus had earlier said: *that they were going to row to the opposite side of the water!*

Do you realize that Jesus wants us to imitate the same peace and dynamic authority that He demonstrated to His friends that day? It's true! As Christians, the Bible assures us that we have the same power within us that Jesus had on earth. He wants us to witness His power to others. He wants even more for us to witness His love to all people!

We are truly living in times that are stretching people. These times are very dark and most people don't have answers to their problems. They may voice their opinion about the world's problems, but have no answers to their personal problems. Worse still, most people are facing a lost eternity because they lack correct knowledge about the Gospel message. Therefore, many people don't understand the reason for their living. They lack purpose in life. The majority of people are just going through the grind of earning a living and trying to do their best in life. People place blame onto others for their heartaches and problems in life. However, the actions of others are only part of the problem.

Mankind's biggest problem is self-centeredness: this is when we are constantly focused on ourselves and our particular wants or problems. Even a little baby is like that! Human nature IS obsessed with itself! All of us have the natural ability to be selfish and to only think of ourselves.

In contrast, if a committed believer demonstrates God's peace and authority, they will also exhibit the attributes of understanding, love and compassion during these hard times. Know that every person who is tuned into the Holy Spirit can make a huge difference in this world!

For example: If you are just one of many people who are employed by an angry boss and you remain peaceful during a storm at work, then that peace stands out – it makes a difference in the minds of the other employees and even in the mind of the boss.

I have had a friend for about six years, ever since I've lived in my suburb. He's attracted to men and in the time that I've known him, he's had a few boyfriends. He's definitely gay. Once, I came in after a couple of years of being his neighbor, I was carrying my Bible and he said, "Your lot doesn't like our lot."

I said to him, "What? In your statement, 'your lot doesn't like our lot,' I assume that you're talking about Christians not liking homo-sexuals. I therefore assume that you're gay. I was not sure about that before, but your statement seems to confirm that you are. Is that what you're saying? You think that because I am a Christian that I don't like gay people?"

He responded, "That's right!"

I replied, "Well, I'm not going to verbally address your statement at the moment because you wouldn't believe me. But you just observe my life. Look at me over the coming years and see if I treat you any differently because you are gay. See if my attitude or love towards you changes in the coming years when we're dealing with each other, or see if it stays the same now that I know you're gay. Let *that* be the judge of whether Christians love you and whether Jesus loves you."

On reflection, that was a very wise answer, something that the Holy Spirit must have given me at the time, because I'm not normally that smart. Well, our relationship has gone on for years. Not too long ago, the same guy came to me and said, "Can you pray for me?"

I asked, "Is there anything specific you want me to pray for?"

He said, "Yes. At the moment, I'm looking for an apartment, but I'm running out of time. I soon have to be out of my present place and I need to find another apartment with suitable roommates. I really am worried. Can you pray that I soon find what I am looking for?"

I said, "Sure, I can pray for that."

Within a week, he came back to me, and with a big grin, he said, "Thanks for your prayers. I've found an apartment with some good roommates."

I replied, "That's great news. I prayed for that."

He was very thankful. Now, here's a person who previously believed that Christians wouldn't love or accept him.

After years of just loving him and being a friend to him, he's asking me for prayer. By this request, he's really saying that he believes that there's a God who listens to Matthew. Therefore, maybe God can actually make a difference in his own life? His prayer request very definitely proved to me that he believes I have special access to God and I can in fact go as an ambassador to appeal to Him on his behalf, according to his personal need. That's awesome!

That's what God wants you to be! He wants you to stand out and dare to be different from other people in this world. As I said before, most people are just consumed with their own problems and passions.

About twenty years ago, I was at a technical college learning to be a chef, when this girl who was a friend in the same course, came to me and said, "Can you pray for me?"

I said, "What about?"

She said, "I just want you to pray for my need. God already knows about it."

I prayed for her. She came up to me a couple of weeks later and said, "Everything's fine now. Thanks for praying."

I asked, "May I ask what it was?"

She paused briefly and then replied, "I thought I was pregnant, but I'm all right now. Everything's okay. Thanks for praying."

Why is it that these two people felt the need to come back to me and thank me for my prayers?

Was it just common courtesy that they came back to me when it seemed that their prayers had been answered? Or was it more that they had respect for the God that is in me? Do they honor and respect the glory of God that is over my life? I think it's the latter. I think that they inwardly respected the God that's part of my life; they wanted to honor Him by thanking me for taking their petition to Him on their behalf.

What part can you play in the Great Commission? You can be the heart of Jesus Christ. You can be His voice, His hands and His feet.

Every believer is to be actively involved in the Great Commission simply by reflecting the love and grace of Jesus to people they meet.

I am the only one of four children in our family who completed Year 12 at High School, but I am not a scholar! I have always been a people-person. Others may view me as quite strange, because I don't wear a mask – I just say things as how they are in my life. If I say things that are hard for you to accept - then that's okay. I am what I am and I know that God loves me for just being me.

Having said that, I want to tell you that Jesus sits on a throne in Heaven, and sometimes He comes down and visits me in visions. I have sometimes met Him in the flesh and interacted with Him, but these are rare occurrences. I don't know if there are heaps of people who have experienced Jesus like I have. Most of the time, however, Jesus is in Heaven when I am interacting with Him.

Jesus has no physical hands to put around that mother in your church who is battling with a husband addicted to gambling or alcohol. Jesus is depending on you to physically hug and encourage her. Nor will Jesus physically give her twenty dollars for the groceries she desperately needs. Jesus loves her, but He has commissioned His believers to act on His behalf. Therefore, Christians need to physically demonstrate their belief in the Savior at every opportunity that presents itself.

Do you realize that what many people in the world calls "evangelism" is just bad news! I say this because some zealous believers major on the "fear of going to hell" instead of God's awesome love in their Gospel presentation. Fear can cause a person to become a religious hypocrite who talks one thing and does another. Their polluted version of "Christianity" will discredit the Gospel in the eyes of the world.

Always bear in mind that the average non-believer has a negative view about Christianity, considering it to be either a belief system that is delusional i.e. a fairy tale, or else, a belief system that is simply used as a spiritual crutch in their life.

Therefore, never try to explain a religious "belief system" to an unbeliever. Instead, *present to them the Living Christ within you!* God's desire is for you to personally demonstrate in your everyday life that Christians are genuine down-to-earth people. In other words, be the type of person that others would themselves like to be. We need to woo people to Jesus, not scare them!

Unbelievers have the same issues and troubles to deal with as believers, but they probably have a little less peace and less understanding and compassion within them. They really struggle to handle negative day-to-day situations in their life. If they know that you're a Christian, they will certainly be watching you. They're watching to see how you handle difficult problems. They're also watching to see if you participate in nasty gossip or laugh at the wrong things.

Unbelievers are constantly watching whether or not you speak harshly to others or watching for your reaction when something goes wrong. They're watching your response when you have been told about a desperate financial need. They're secretly hoping that your faith in God will allow you to give money towards that need. They're pleasantly surprised when you do that.

There are all kinds of genuine needs in people's lives and Jesus wants you to help in any way you can. By doing this, you may discover that you were actually part of the pathway leading to someone's salvation.

What I am saying is that we are not only to pray for the unsaved, but we should put legs on our faith by meeting the needs of others, whenever we can do so.

There are always enough homeless and broken hearted people in a city to minister help and love to. Therefore, there would be plenty of needs in your society if you're willing to get your hands dirty: if you're willing to go into a place that makes you feel uncomfortable. (This is a secret weapon that I have in my own life.)

There would be literally hundreds of different things that you personally could do over a lifetime that would assist in fulfilling the Great Commission. Just be assured that no role or no person is too insignificant for God to mightily use in this enormous task. Jesus once said "The harvest is ripe but the laborers are few," and sadly, over two thousand years later, that's still true today!

One day, I was walking along a street and there was a person who was illuminated to me by the Holy Spirit. All I knew was that this person was male. I walked past initially and finally I agreed to the Holy Spirit to go back. I went back to this guy and said, "Excuse me. I have a gift and sometimes that gift allows me to receive a message for a person. Today, I have been given a message for you, sir. Would you like to hear it?"

He said, "Yes."

Then I said, "You're in a workplace at the moment where the boss is riding you very hard. In fact, only this week, you've been looking in the newspapers for another job.

You really love the work that you're doing and you're very gifted and skilled at it, but you can't handle the pressure coming from your boss, nor his attitude. You wish you could stay at the company, but this man's personality is giving you no choice.

God wants you to know that there is a choice! God wants you to just hang on for the time being. Soon, within six months, there's going to be another job opportunity in your present place of employment. You will soon have the chance to transfer to another department, well away from your present boss.

You are constantly asking yourself: why is this boss in my life? God wants you to know that He has allowed this man to be part of your life. He wants you to know that one day, you're going to be a part of management and supervision. He wants you to have a very good example of what not to be! Your boss is under tremendous strain, with deadlines and pressure from upper management and he simply can't handle the stress. The only way he can handle his stress is to diffuse his pressure and anger onto others.

God wants you to handle and demonstrate a good character even while you're under stress. So He's giving you a very good example of what not to be."

The gentleman was really surprised and I asked, "Does that make sense?" His girlfriend was nodding her head – yes!

The guy put his hand up and shook my hand. He simply said, "Thank you so much for your message."

I replied, "God Bless you. I pray that everything works out for you. Have a good day," and I walked off.

Now, that's the part you can play in a person's life.

When you look at that particular situation, it was crucial that he had the right choice. God wanted him to continue in that job. Within six months, God plans to bless him with a new job. God wanted him to transfer and continue to work for the same good firm. He wanted him to do the work that he really enjoys but He didn't want him having the pressure of looking for another job.

God had used my lips to give the man an understanding as to why that particular boss was allowed in his life. The man's heartfelt questions were answered and he received direction in his life as well.

I'll very briefly take apart this prophecy and share what elements there are in it. A lot of that prophecy was Word of Knowledge. Some of it was the Word of Wisdom and some of it was prophecy. We'll look at all three elements in later chapters of this book.

Did that guy need to be saved in that instance? Did he need to be led into the sinner's prayer or did God already impact him with a life-affirming message of hope and encouragement for his life now? You see, Jesus isn't sitting up in Heaven wishing everyone would immediately become a Christian! God is not impatient! No, He is a perfect gentleman and He has His own plans and timeframe for bringing people to salvation.

Don't feel under any obligation or pressure to "save" a person when you give them a prophetic word. Just deliver to them what they need at the time – if they're thirsty, give them water. If they're suffering, give them an aid to their suffering. If there's a message to give, pass it on. All the messages from God are meant to encourage and inspire people and to make the person's life a little better.

Actually, a person who gives prophecies to others is someone who's giving life-giving water to thirsty people. Would you deny water to a thirsty person? If you had access to it, would you not give it to them? I pray that this message has encouraged you. Discover for yourself by asking God what part you can play in the Great Commission.

three

Learning To Be a Light

How can we learn to be a light? Isn't a light something you turn on with a switch and it appears? Well, it is essentially like that, but you can learn to practice to become a much brighter light just like as if you had a dimmer switch.

Imagine that you have a dimmer switch on your personal life and this light of yours can shine brighter according to the Holy Spirit's working on you. You see, the Holy Spirit has a part in every Christian's life, but the Holy Spirit's part actually depends on how much of a person's life is given over to Jesus Christ, that is, how much of that person's life is really surrendered to Him.

All of us have hidden compartments in our life that God wants access to. Many people have a compartment for money, which they keep closed off to God. This is basically because they don't believe God is the supplier of all their needs. They justify their reluctance, because of their lack of knowledge about God's principles when it comes to money. When the financial compartment is shut off, it will limit the light that can impact others in their local community.

In some way, we all can influence people we know and interact with daily. Do you realize that it's mostly the "fear of lack" that stops people from being generous with their money? For example, when you have this type of fear and you only have three dollars in your pocket, you will hang onto it. If a stranger comes up and asks you for some spare change, you will not give it to them. You will dim your conscience by thinking something like "they'll probably spend it on drugs or alcohol."

Not only do you have that reason not to give money, your fear of lack will convince you that you actually need that money in your pocket! When in fact, you could probably have operated in love and given at least one of those dollars to the person who asked for help. This is just one way that the brightness of your light can be affected by that inner compartment regarding money.

Do you realize that you can develop a tremendous love for people of other faiths, if you are financially contributing to certain ministries - for example: if some of your money is going towards a Christian radio ministry that broadcasts to Muslim countries, then part of you takes an interest in understanding Muslims. In time, you may even find your heart open to giving *more* money to that ministry.

Perhaps as your love grows, you may even read the Quran and take an interest in getting to know what they actually believe. Giving to Muslim ministries impacts our money compartment! If this compartment for money is closed, well then, the light that you could shine in that particular area is switched off.

On a personal note, if a Christian believes that God isn't good enough to supply a perfect partner for them, one who will enrich and bless their life, then they will be a person who's always looking for love in the wrong places. Essentially, let's come to the understanding that only the person who's meant to be with you is the right person! Any other method of looking for a spouse, aside from waiting on God to supply that person, is looking at the wrong place.

Therefore, I am saying that you don't have to be an immoral and a promiscuous person to be looking at the wrong place. I believe that you are looking at the wrong place when you're not waiting on God. If that "romance compartment" in your life isn't handed over and submitted to God, then that too, can affect your light and how you interact with people.

I will give you an example of this: If you are a single female, you may have a few single men who are attracted to you, and that you are currently flirting with. People can say that flirting is innocent fun and shouldn't be taken seriously, but flirting can negatively affect a single person when another shows him or her wrong signals. Then, if he or she moves forward by these false signals, the innocent party who has believed the signals is emotionally injured. Know that this type of practice will affect your light.

In fact, every compartment in your life that is not surrendered and given to God will affect your light. Therefore, the more of your life surrendered and submitted to God, the more His Holy Spirit can show His light through you. Always know that we are called to be ambassadors for Christ – this is a high calling, but we have God's power within us to fulfill it.

Twenty years ago, I was walking down a street and what looked like a homeless man approached me and asked me if I had any spare change. Well, I had a five dollar note on me, but I would have had to go to a shop to change it because I needed three dollars to spend on milk and bread. But I couldn't be bothered changing the note, so I said to the homeless man that I didn't have any spare change. I lied. I did have spare change, but I just couldn't be bothered going to the effort of changing it.

When I said: "No!" the Holy Spirit said to my spirit, "*What you do to the least of my brethren, you do unto Me.*" I turned around and ran back to where the guy was. He'd gone behind a phone booth and when I got there, he had disappeared into thin air. I looked more than a hundred feet from the phone booth in every direction. There was no one to be seen. The actual man had disappeared into thin air and I couldn't understand it.

I continued walking up the street and a guy approached me at a set of lights, where people in the past have asked me for directions. This man did ask me for directions to a particular street. Being a taxi driver at the time, it was no problem to assist him.

Then he said, "Let me give you this," and he handed me a ten dollar note.

I replied, "I can't take that!"

He said, "Yes, you saved me. My time is very important just now!"

Then he went off. Now, I'm not sure if this second man was an angel, but I'm sure that the man who disappeared into thin air, *must* have been an angel in disguise!

Now, I had been given ten dollars after I had refused a needy person just five dollars. I started to cry because I was feeling so guilty. I said to Jesus, "I'm sorry."

Jesus answered, "You judged that first man! You said to yourself that he was a drunk and he's probably going to spend it on drink. Because you judged him, you didn't give him your spare change. You need to stop judging people Matthew. You need to *learn* to stop this habit, so I can share my love more clearly through you. If you give to me, I'll always supply your needs. I'll always look after you."

There are two elements in this story. First, I judged the person. Second, I had a fear of lack because I had not trusted God to supply my needs.

That fear had prevented me from giving away my original money. If I had given it away, I still would have been in the same place to receive the other ten dollars. So, it's not that God wouldn't have supplied my need. No, it was my fear of lack and my judgmental attitude that was my problem.

God has specifically told us certain things. For example: We are told not to judge others. We are also told to obey what Jesus taught. Some of the things He taught us were: to forgive people, to bless them, to go the extra mile for them, to turn the other cheek and to stand out and be different to the average person in the world.

God doesn't want us to just have head knowledge about the teachings of His Son.

God wants us to know these teachings in order to be able to obey them. It says in the Great Commission, "*Teaching them to observe all the things I've commanded you: and lo, I'll be with you to the end of the age,*" says Matthew 28:20. To be a light in this world, we have to obey Jesus. To be an effective witness to unbelievers, we must set our benchmark very high – we have to be like Jesus, the Son of God! God wants every Christian to be Jesus on Earth to all they meet.

I'll share some of my tips. When you're going out into life and you're interacting with people, it's quite easy to smile at a person and briefly say: "Hello" even if they're strangers. It's even easy to smile and say, "Hello. How's your day?" But pause slightly as you say it so that they can respond if they want to. It's hypercritical if you say it and don't slow down a bit.

On the other hand, if someone greets you like this, dig deeper than the customary response of, "Fine." Ask God to heighten your awareness to be pro-active in developing conversations. He will do that for you because He wants you to be His light to others. To be a light, you just want to give people a positive experience in their day: for them to feel acknowledged in a good way. That's just one simple way to demonstrate your light. It's very easy and it can become a habit!

I want you to know that servers, whether male or female, are people who work hard with customer after customer and they're not necessarily having a good day. Someone's eggs weren't cooked right; so-and-so expects their cup to be always full even though they drink at an alarming rate and the noisy three-year-old at table two keeps dumping his spaghetti onto the walkway! It takes an outstanding person to have a good day all day long, serving customers.

Now, every time you go into a restaurant and be served, you can ask them, "How has your day been?" Listen to what they say and respond with an encouraging word. You could say, "The day will be over soon." Or perhaps, "It'll be good to spend your money at the end of the week" or "All of us only work to pay the bills, and God Bless!"

It's so easy to interact with people who are servers. Say simple things like: "Thank you." "Please." "Have a wonderful day!" "I hope all your greatest dreams come true." Try to make it a practice to bless the people you interact with, especially those who are serving you. To do so, you only need to shine your light into their situation.

It's easy too, to build a healthy, friendly relationship with the people you meet in the various shops you go to. I find that most people love to be recognized. I know that I love to be! By taking an interest in others, they will likely take an interest in you and maybe even what you believe. We really do have many opportunities to shine God's light.

My personal and favorite way of approaching strangers, if God leads me, is to share a prophetic word that He has for them.

I am sure that most people inwardly appreciate being acknowledged in some way and it's totally non-threatening to casually ask them how their day is. There are people who serve you all over the place. Also, there are people that you sit next to, on a bus or on a train. You can remain aloof and indifferent like everyone else. Or you can choose to be different by casually greeting them in a very simple nonthreatening way. It's easy to start up a conversation and you will quickly feel in your spirit if you are infringing on their space. Most people like to talk about their hobbies and interests – I have learned about all sorts of interesting things when listening to others.

A question you can ask is, "What do you do for work?" Asking someone, "How are you doing?" often results in a canned response, but asking about work usually elicits a detailed response and starts a conversation. Then you can ask what do they do to relax and they'll tell you. During the conversation, once they've told you all those things, they'll ask you, "What do you do to relax? What do you do for work?" This is your chance to very briefly share about your life and who knows where the Holy Spirit will lead you.

If you're not interacting with people you meet and who serve you, who are you talking to? Who will give you the opportunity to bring Christ's light to and witness to? This is the way I live my life. I speak to heaps of people as I'm always engaging people in conversations and engaging people with friendly gestures.

I know that the guard's job on the train includes making sure that everyone has safely boarded or departed the train and that all is okay on the station. Therefore, I know that I'm never going to develop a relationship with the guards that are on all my trains because there are hundreds of them, but I always lift my eyebrows and say, "Hello," to a guard on the subway as I get off.

Just letting them know that you're happy with their service blesses a person. You see, the Holy Spirit is pretty smart. Never underestimate Him: He knows how to sow a thought into a person, like: "He's very friendly, I wonder if he's friendly like that to everyone."

As I have said a few times, the Holy Spirit is very smart. It's up to us to be the light. Think of ways you can connect with people and to bless them. You don't have to be someone who you're not, but let the Christ in you shine!

Let's be someone who asks others about their needs and to do something about them, even if it's just taking the time to listen. God wants you to be a blessing. He doesn't want you to be just another selfish person looking out for yourself. He wants access to every part of your life. He wants you to give every part of your life to Him.

I'd encourage you to sit down and make a list of the parts of your life that God doesn't presently have access to and I'd ask you to prayerfully consider giving Him that access. I'd like to now finish with a sample prayer.

"Father, I ask that you start to show me the areas in my life that I need to surrender to You. Illuminate those areas for me and give me the courage and the power through the Holy Spirit to release those areas to you.

Father, I want to be a better light in my community for I know that You deeply love every person. Show me how to be a better light and lead me by your Holy Spirit exactly what to do and say always. In Jesus' name I ask, Amen."

four

Understanding Seeds

In the New Testament, Jesus talks about "seeds" quite often. We need to understand the principle of the seeds.

Have you ever stopped to think that every seed is already dead when it's placed into the ground? This is a mystery! I don't know how seeds can come back to life when they're in the ground dead, but apparently, even though they are dead, they come back to life and grow into something different. That's the way God has designed all seeds to be!

You may not completely understand the process of seeds, but hopefully as a child or sometime when you were growing up, you planted a seed in a piece of dirt and had the experience of growing a little plant.

If you haven't had that personal experience, just believe that seeds, if they're planted in the right spot, in the right soil and given some water and sunshine, will eventually sprout and grow into a little plant that will grow bigger and bigger until you replant it or put it elsewhere so its roots can go deeper. In other words, it will grow into whatever type of plant that God originally ordained it to be.

I want to discuss seeds just for a little while, for you to understand that the world is filled with people whom you can plant a "spiritual" seed into and then see it germinate! You may not necessarily have the privilege to actually see it germinate, but I want you to always have faith in

God that it will eventually germinate in His set time. For example: When I mentioned in an earlier chapter about a guy who had a hard boss and I said he would get a promotion, I planted a "*seed of hope*" in his life.

I planted that seed and encouraged him to stay in his present job and not to make a decision that God didn't want him to make. Now, that guy wasn't a Christian, but God was still concerned with his life and wanted him to make the right decision. God didn't want him to go to an outside job because He wanted to bless him in a new job within his current firm. God is very interested in the lives of all people.

At times, it's hard to understand that God is intimately concerned with the lives of all people!

Sometimes, after attending church regularly for many years, we might begin to believe that God is really only interested in His believers – what they are doing or experiencing. Many times, unfortunately, we can insulate ourselves from the people of the world. We can even lose sight of the Great Commission and adopt the understanding that God really isn't interested in blessing people who aren't Christians! Now that's a very sad place to be!

Some Christians confidently say that God knows which people are going to give their lives to Jesus and they quote scriptures to confirm this. Therefore, they presume that God isn't really concerned about people whom He knows are not ever going to give their lives to Jesus.

Let me tell you that God is concerned with every single person. His love is not based on their belief structure. God has love for even the worst sinner! He has both love and compassion for them! Jesus died on the cross for every person born since time began.

God was concerned with the man who hated his boss! God had a definite plan for his life. Therefore, God planted a "seed of hope" in his life regarding future employment. In God's due time, the job opportunity would be advertised in his workplace and when the man applies for it, he would secure the job. That's really a germination of that seed.

That man would have remembered my words to him and I can picture him thinking and saying to himself: "It's amazing. I'm so glad I stayed in my job." I can identify with this man myself, because the Holy Spirit brings thoughts of the past into my mind all the time.

The Holy Spirit can speak to anyone He chooses to! He hasn't a biased attitude like man. A person doesn't need to be a Christian for God to speak to them and lead them into actions that are good for them. It's crazy to think that only Satan and demons have the right to speak to everyone.

So when this man sees the new job opportunity in his workplace and actually secures it, it's not too hard to believe that the Holy Spirit will remind him that God had made it all happen.

It's very important that you see your prophetic words to people, as being a seed, which God in His appointed time will germinate. Knowing that you have planted a special "seed" gives you courage to step out and be bolder with people. You will be able to use more words of knowledge, and be more confident in prophesying to total strangers. The bottom line is that God is the amazing "Author" of seed sowing and harvest and we know that it's His desire that all should be saved.

Alternatively, if you don't see your prophetic words as living seeds that have a future and a purpose in people's lives, then the prophetic life will become harder and harder for you to continually do without receiving constant encouraging feedback.

I know that there are multitudes of people that one day will be in heaven because of a prophetic word that I gave them. I know that whenever the Lord plants a seed from my lips, that seed is just a tiny step in a series of steps that God will use to bring someone to salvation. Therefore, I am confident that there will be a reward waiting for me in

Heaven. My friends would readily acknowledge that I'm not a person who looks for earthly rewards, but I always look for the greater reward - the reward from my Lord Jesus. I want eternal rewards!

I believe that it's very important for you to understand the following three concepts:

1. Be Jesus to people. Don't try to convert them when the Holy Spirit hasn't moved you.
2. To understand that you're planting seeds in fertile ground. If the Holy Spirit has illuminated a person, then you can be confident that they are fertile ground.
3. It is profitable and amazing for you to understand that your prophetic word is a seed. It says in Isaiah that God's Word doesn't return to Him void. This means that when you give a prophetic word, (*which is a word from God*) to a stranger, it *will* accomplish God's purposes in the life of that stranger.

Even if people forget it for a while, the prophetic word will be brought back to their memory when it starts to be fulfilled.

Many times we've been told something was going to happen, but we somehow just forgot about it for years - until it happens! Then, we will recall that we had been told about it and will hopefully give glory to God. Well, the same thing is true when you plant a seed in the form of a prophetic word, into the life of a stranger. You can be certain that the seed will bear fruit and flourish one day in that person's life.

When you believe and understand that the prophetic word is a seed from God designed by Him to flourish and bear fruit, then you will come to the understanding that it's time to start to use the gift of prophecy as God illuminates various people to you. Faith in the love and goodness of God is the spiritual tap that releases His words into your mind for you to then speak out!

When you really comprehend that you can possibly influence thousands of lives by being obedient to God's leading, you will become very happy with your Christian walk. When you've fully grasped this concept, it will take this book from being an ordinary book, to something personally practiced and applied.

I heard the Holy Spirit say to me once that *Wisdom is the proper application of knowledge.*

The world is full of books and Internet sites. There's so much knowledge about so many subjects, but it's only when we receive knowledge and apply that knowledge practically, that we will become wise. So many people possess knowledge, but fail to personally apply it. Therefore, wisdom slips by them. A wise person makes good decisions because they have personally applied in a practical way the particular knowledge they have gained.

I have tried to make this book on Prophetic Evangelism simple, so that it will be easily understood by all its readers. It's definitely not my desire to just fill people with knowledge that I have learnt. My only desire is that they will read the book and become wise in the subject. That is, that they will actually apply the knowledge within this book.

However, if you read this book and enjoy its contents and then pass it on to your friends so that they can be encouraged by the stories and the subject matter, then, that is still a good thing

My earnest hope is that the spiritual gifts will be imparted to you and you write to me and prophesy over me so that I can give you feedback to encourage you. It's best that you start to prophesy over Christians in your church and that way, you will gain confidence in your gift, so that soon, you will be able to prophesy over strangers. My dream is that every serious reader will begin to do Prophetic Evangelism in the near future.

That's a little about understanding seeds. I want you to understand that you're a powerful person and you can have a powerful effect on people.

five

The Holy Spirit is Smart.

To the reader, this chapter heading may seem too logical! You may respond and say "Of course, He is smart – He is God! Why is the author writing a whole chapter about that?"

The fact that the Holy Spirit is smart may seem a logical statement to most people, but I, personally, am totally awed by it – the Holy Spirit IS SO smart! Those words come to my mind repeatedly, every day! In fact, I find myself speaking them out to people all the time. The wisdom of the Holy Spirit will never stop amazing me.

The fact of the matter is that many Christians don't actually believe that truth! These Christians don't understand or believe that the Holy Spirit is a genius, because if they did comprehend just how smart He is, they would do what the He tells them to do. They would obey Him!

If people knew that the message and the commands that Jesus brought to us were smart, they will obey them. If they understood that the best way to live was the way that Jesus proposed, they'd live that way! If people truly believed that Jesus was right, they'd live the right way. It's because we are so selfish that we live our lives in a self-centered way.

We assume that we know better and essentially, that type of arrogance is the basis for sin in the world! Sin is doing things your way and not doing things God's way. Jesus clearly laid down the way that we should live if we are to be His followers. He says quite plainly in John

14:21, "If you love me, obey my commands." Jesus is very serious about us obeying Him.

His instructions in the Great Commission to his disciples includes: "*Teaching them to observe all the things I've commanded you,*" in Matthew 28:20. Obeying the commandments of Jesus is mentioned about seven times in the books of John alone. Why is it repeated so many times? Because people simply don't do it! I believe that Jesus and the Holy Spirit allowed this message "to obey" to be repeated so many times in the New Testament, because He knew that we would be reluctant to do so.

If you think that the Holy Spirit isn't smart, then you'll try to do the Holy Spirit's work for Him.

For example: If there is a man in your church who is a practicing gay, you would probably consider it your duty to tell him that he is living a life of sin.

Now, at the risk of ruffling some feathers, I want to say at this point: The Holy Spirit doesn't always need you to point out sin in the lives of others.

Please note that I said "doesn't always need." I did not say: "doesn't ever need." I'm mindful of the context of 1 Corinthians Chapter 5 regarding immoral behavior within a Christian congregation. There are strict rules that apply, but this book is not about that. I just want to point out to you that you should not make it your job to condemn others.

Why do I say this? I say it because the Holy Spirit is pretty smart at convicting people and showing them their sin. He knows when a particular person is going to give their life to Jesus. He knows when a believer is ready and able to receive His prompting about sin. The Holy Spirit simply knows everything and He can do anything!

He also knows which of you reading this book will pray the impartation prayer; will practice their new gift on Christians; will practice their gifts on me for feedback and then start to walk in Prophetic Evangelism.

The Holy Spirit knows how popular or unpopular this book is going to be. He already knows every person who's going to benefit from this book and live a changed life because of it. He knows now whether you're going to take this message and run with it or if you're just going to put this message on a shelf for the time being – perhaps even years!

If you decide to shelve it for the time being, He's smart enough to know when to encourage you to read it again, because He already knows the person you will direct your first message to and what date that will be. He has perfect timing always – He never gets it wrong!

I am totally confident in His awesome ability to change lives. You can relax and know that if you're reading and enjoying this book, you can and will prophesy over people. In fact, many of you will walk in the gift of Prophetic Evangelism and witness to strangers. The Holy Spirit is smart! He knows if you're going to do it in the near future or whether you're going to procrastinate. He knows the people who will never do it. He even knows the people who will advertise this book to all their Christian friends.

He knows how many thousands of people are going to become effective in Prophetic Evangelism. The Holy Spirit knew in advance the things I was going to share in this book. All I had in my head were the chapter headings and a video camera. I actually spoke this book and then painstakingly worked on it to make it a readable book for others to enjoy.

So, with the understanding that the Holy Spirit understands every-thing, we can continue.

The Holy Spirit knows all the people He wants to use you to give a prophetic word to. He will have people in your city coming across your path all the time: people that He wants you to share with. He will have people lined up to sit next to you on a bus, or train, or at the theatre, a shopping center or whatever. He will organize meetings in every type of place imaginable and it will just happen! You will become like me and constantly say to others: "The Holy Spirit is smart, you know!"

He has every detail planned. He can change the plans of a person, or have them delayed in some way, so that certain people meet at the right place at the exact same time. Bear in mind, the Holy Spirit isn't just working on setting the scene right, He is more importantly, working with the players in the scene. You need to be in the anointing - in the right frame of mind to deliver a prophetic word. The other person needs to be receptive, to what is going to be presented to them.

He will illuminate to you the person to whom you are to approach. He will put His anointing in your voice. He gives His power to the message at the precise moment you begin to speak out the prophetic word. Because of God's anointing on His word, it will make a definite impression on the hearer, even if no immediate feedback is given!

I want you to be assured that every time you prophesy, the Holy Spirit will be riding on the message you deliver to people. God had already illuminated the person for you in some way, so be confidently at rest, that your words fell on fertile ground!

You know, sometimes you can be listening to a sermon and one sentence that the preacher says makes an impact on you and you really take it aboard – it's like a new revelation to you and you ponder on it. The Holy Spirit was riding on that sentence when it came to you. Now, the Holy Spirit rides on certain sentences according to specific people in the congregation. A preacher will preach and the Holy Spirit touches people according to their circumstance and maturity in the Lord. The whole congregation hears the message but they don't all hear it the same way!

I want you to know that the Holy Spirit not only rides on the message that you give, He oversees that person's life and arranges for situations in their life to work together, in such a way that the prophetic word spoken to them will come true. The Holy Spirit works on that word: He touches the person's life and reminds them that the prophetic word was true and that it really came from a loving God, who is very interested in them and their situation.

Now that you know that the Holy Spirit is smart, the first thing to do is to give your life to Him and surrender every part of your life. Ask the Holy Spirit to show you things in your life that are not yet surrendered, or not yet completely surrendered to Him and surrender these things to Him.

The second thing to do is to continue reading this book. I pray that after reading the impartation chapter, that you will respond to it. I encourage ALL of you, who pray the impartation prayer, to practice your gift. Write to me and prophesy over me and let me confirm to you that your prophecy was right. Rather than putting down the book and not doing it, just take that chance and actually prophesy over me and discover that you have a real gift. My feedback will be both positive and honest, I promise you.

Simply ask the Holy Spirit to give you a message for someone in your church and the Holy Spirit will give it to you. Then you take that next step and give the message to that particular person. Just say to them: "The Lord has laid something on my heart for you, can I share it?" Then you share it with them. You don't have to say it's a "prophecy." You don't have to say it's a special word from God.

You just say that the Holy Spirit laid something on your heart and you share it with them. When you prophesy, and receive feedback, then you'll know you have received the gift. After a few practices, you can go into the further stages of taking it to the streets.

The Holy Spirit knows in advance what He's doing in your life. He is deeply concerned with your life. Whether you run with the gift now, or run with it in the future or even if you never run with it - God wants you to know that He loves you. God wants you to know that He adores you and that you're extremely precious to Him. This isn't a case of whether some people can do it and some people can't. Every person can do it – we have God's Word on it!

You may ask, "How can I be so sure of this?

It says in the book of Revelation that Jesus is the spirit of prophecy. So everyone who has Jesus in their life can prophesy. It's not hard to prophesy.

Prophecy is simply sharing with someone a message that Jesus has laid on your heart for them and Christians do that all the time. You do that without even thinking. You feel that you have something to say to a person and you say it to them and it really encourages them. You basically just prophesied to a person. Just because you didn't say it came from God doesn't mean you haven't been used by the Holy Spirit to minister to a person through love and compassion.

So I hope that you understand that the Holy Spirit is smart. You can start to prove it before long by doing what He puts on your heart to do. Show Him that He's the boss and show Him that you're willing to move according to how He wants you to move.

six

Walking with the Holy Spirit

One of the best ways of walking with the Holy Spirit is to obey both the commands and directions of Jesus Christ. To obey His commands, you have to first know what they are.

It's one thing to say that you're a Christian; it's another thing to walk like Jesus would have you walk. The commands of Jesus are essentially impossible for the natural man to do. Therefore, in order to do so, we must move into the realm of the Holy Spirit. Only His power within us will enable us to do it. Constantly relying on His power within us is to be walking in the Holy Spirit

For example, when a person on Facebook posts an unkind statement about you, you will be able to retaliate by the Spirit and not by the flesh. The advice of Jesus is to first forgive and then to turn the other cheek.

We can all place boundaries in our life: we set these boundaries to basically protect us. We can put up boundaries in our relationships, particularly with outsiders. Jesus doesn't want us to put ourselves in a position to be abused by anyone. However, if abuse of any kind occurs, He asks us to forgive the offender and to turn the other cheek and to pray for them. I found personally that when I've had enemies, it's helpful to pray for them, because as you start to invest time and resources into doing this, you start to come to respect them differently.

Walking in the Holy Spirit is an absolute essential part of Prophetic Evangelism. So many times, I've had a feeling to go down to the shopping center and do my shopping at a particular time. I've gone to the shopping center and there's been a person whom the Lord has wanted me to approach and they have just been sitting on a seat as I walked into the store.

Now, half an hour before that, they probably weren't sitting in the seat and often times, five minutes after I delivered God's message to them, they're not sitting on the seat anymore. So how did I arrive at the mall at the right time to speak to them? I had moved through my intuition, through the leading of the Holy Spirit. The Holy Spirit often speaks to us through our intuition.

Perhaps, your intuition says to you: "It's a good time to go shopping" and if you first disagree with what your mind says, the thought will come up again, "wouldn't it be best to go shopping now and get it out of the way." Several promptings may come into your mind when the Holy Spirit is leading you to do something.

We need to become spiritually aware of these things, especially when we want to be used by the Holy Spirit in Prophetic Evangelism. A very simple example would be: when you come into a shop and you see a worker who has a long queue waiting, the Holy Spirit might impress upon you to say something like, "Work is busy today, isn't it?" Or perhaps, "It must be hard to serve so many people."

You see, it's so easy to blend in with other people, but the Holy Spirit wants you to develop the habit of being aware of others, all the time, so He will often place thoughts in your mind concerning them. By obeying His promptings, you will be walking in the Holy Spirit. Nothing escapes God's attention and we too are to be constantly aware of the people around us.

Bear in mind that thoughts come to the human mind by three different sources:

- You can just think your own thought, which comes from your personal soul area. For example: "She seems to be a lovely girl. I wish I knew her."

- Satan can bring a thought into your mind like, "There's a beautiful girl. Go over and chat with her and who knows where it will lead!"

- The Holy Spirit can quietly say, "That girl over there really needs to hear from Me."

Sometimes, in the flesh, that is, our soul area, we unconsciously make judgments about people according to their appearance. God doesn't want us to do that! We must always know that people whom we consider to be handsome or beautiful has a need to be encouraged and shown God's love, just like anyone else. The same is true for those whom we consider successful in life. Therefore, I have found that it's very important to try to not pre-judge people or put them in a box of our own making. This is especially true when it comes to prophetic evangelism.

Once, for example, I saw this attractive girl at McDonald's. The Holy Spirit spoke to me about her, but at the time I thought my own mind had created the thought. Later on, I had another look at her and once again, I presumed my own soul was drawn to her beauty.

Then, when the third time my eyes glanced in her direction, I said to the Holy Spirit, "Do you want me to say something to her?"

God said, "Yes. Tell her that she's been constantly praying to me for a particular situation. She believes in the parable in the Bible, that if she is persistent with her prayers, that I will give in and grant her request. She's continually pleading for a particular thing to happen. Tell her that I'm not going to grant her request. My reason is that I want to make room for something better in her life than what she is requesting of me. Tell her that what I have prepared is far better!"

From that prophetic word, I could tell that she was a Christian, because she had been praying. I went over and told her what I had received.

The Holy Spirit had shared with me, the basic approach line written about earlier in this book. I approach a person and I'll say, "Excuse me." They look at me and I will continue, "I have a gift and from time-to-time that gift allows me to give a certain message to someone. Today, just now, I received a message for you. Would you like to hear it?" Most times, even up to ninety nine percent of the time, people agree and I give them the message.

So I gave her the message and she was very thankful for it.

Often, after you've shared with a person and they begin to walk away, they will look over at you and wave or smile. On this particular occasion, the girl just got up and left without waving or acknowledging me in any way. I was put out a little, thinking that she wasn't appreciative and I heard Jesus say to me: "Acknowledgment isn't the important thing, Matthew. The important thing is for her to have heard the message. We finally found someone who would approach her and deliver our message. Thank you for doing that, so Matthew, accept My thanks instead!"

Another time, I was walking down the street and I saw a homeless guy and he had a cup for change. I knelt and I put a five dollar note in the change container and he didn't acknowledge me by thanking me. Once again, I walked off a little put out by his complacency in not even acknowledging or thanking me.

Jesus said, "Are you upset that he didn't acknowledge you?"

I said, "Yes."

He said, "Well, what you do to the least of my brethren, you do unto me. So I want to personally thank you, Matthew, for giving me your five dollar note."

I almost filled up with tears.

Sometimes, people move in the immature stages of a gift and at times I still do! Sometimes, I admit that I move in the prophetic, for what I can get out of it. I want to receive thanks from people, or at least be thanked for the message. Often, people will recognize the same characteristic in themselves, when they give a compliment to a person and hope for the person to respond with a 'thank you.' I know that both of these things have been true in my own life.

If we are honest, we all at times do good things out of selfish motives. We like to be acknowledged and encouraged that we're doing a good job. I am personally of the opinion that there are some really zealous Christians doing outstanding works for the kingdom of God, but they are doing them from a wrong motive.

We must be ever mindful that God never wants us to do good works out of a sense of duty, because that motive comes from a religious mindset. Our love for God and our desire to be a blessing to those He loves should always be our attitude regarding works! So we must always check the motive for our actions.

The Holy Spirit will start to increase His manifestations in your life, as you start to act on the impressions that come into your mind. As you increase doing this, the Holy Spirit will increase the times that He speaks and directs you. When you're a little more skilled, the Holy Spirit will direct you with just a quick thought. He'll say, "Go and do your shopping now" rather than intuitively thinking "It would be a good time to do my shopping now."

The Holy Spirit will increase His directness to you by saying something like: "It's time to do your shopping. There's someone I want you to meet." Or He'll just say to you, "Do your shopping now!" It's best to agree with that and go and do it.

I have now basically covered that obeying Jesus and acting in the character of Jesus, by obeying what He taught, is one way to move in the Holy Spirit. Certainly, to obey what Jesus taught requires super-strength. In fact, no human can do it. Therefore, to walk in what Jesus taught, you need to walk in the enabling power of the Holy Spirit.

Also, be very aware of your intuition regarding your thoughts and words, because most times it's the Holy Spirit who is directing you.

It's not uncommon for me to tell a man that he has a nice tie on or he has a nice shirt on. It's not uncommon for me to tell a girl that she has a pretty dress on. I seem to compliment people very often. Why do I do this? It's because I make it my business to really look at people. I don't just glance at them like they didn't matter. I know that this habit of mine is the work of the Holy Spirit in me. He wants me to notice people all the time, because He notices them! They are all very precious and uniquely special in His eyes.

Therefore, I'm very confident that any compliments coming from me are moves of the Holy Spirit. God is actually speaking through me to encourage and lift a person's spirit.

I believe that every Christian's actions are a display of Jesus Christ to the unsaved world. You are His witness. Therefore, I challenge you to be a weapon for righteousness. It's a sad, bad world! It's dark, depressing and lonely. People on the whole are selfish: they are so self-focused and self-interested, that they are surprised and even shocked, when someone comes along with no hidden agenda to show love, compassion, and understanding to them or others.

The light of Christ in you can do marvelous things. I want you to know that God wants to move in you, and He also wants to move through you by His Holy Spirit, by giving you directions through your intuition. I pray that this chapter has been very helpful for you.

seven

What is Evangelism?

Is evangelism something you see in a huge tent crusade? Or is it a special local church event, held perhaps monthly? Yes, evangelism would definitely occur in both of these cases. An evangelical event is organized by Christians in order to attract non-believers to a meeting to hear the Gospel message explained in a simple and relevant way.

However, it may surprise you but most people who become a Christian, don't do so through that style of evangelizing. The majority of people become a Christian through the personal witness and the example of another Christian who is in their life. Therefore, we must be always aware that unbelievers are closely watching those who claim that Jesus Christ is their Lord and Savior.

I believe that unbelievers are judging for themselves: "Is Matthew's God authentic? Does this Jesus that Matthew talks about watch over me like he watches over him?" Know that unbelievers are watching *you* and they're measuring *your* God through the actions that *you* take and the things that *you* do! Therefore, Biblical evangelism is actually being Christ in your neighborhood, or being Christ in the community that you interact with. Evangelism is doing the works of Christ, as you are able and equipped to do. I said before that giving some money to people in need is an extremely practical way of showing people your light.

I'm on a disability pension, yet it's surprising how much money I have. I am constantly amazed that on average, I can spend two hundred dollars evey two weeks, on things of God and producing my books and giving to other ministries. I say this not to build myself up, but to simply acknowledge what is true in my life. I have often pondered about finances. It's amazing how much spare money you have when you're not just spending it on superfluous things. Before I started writing books, I did waste quite a bit of money doing things that were not very beneficial to me.

Evangelism is living the life of Jesus Christ. Evangelism is not saying to unbelievers that when they die, they're going to hell! That type of news just feeds fear into someone. Fear is one of Satan's favorite tools! Fear and not faith, could lead an unbeliever into saying a sinner's prayer when they have no intention of surrendering their life to the Lord Jesus Christ. Fear causes such a person to live a hypercritical life, which in turn, causes other unbelievers to resist Christianity and the devil wins big time!

In Australia, most people hate being preached at. I don't know how it is in America, but in Australia, the average person you meet firmly believes that if they're not a pedophile or a murderer, that they are Heaven bound. Ninety-nine percent of non-Christians believe that Heaven will welcome them, while only one percent boasts of going to Hell and partying with their mates.

Most Australians believe essentially, that someone would have to be very evil to not go to Heaven. They certainly don't believe that they have to give their lives to Jesus Christ and to actually have a personal relationship with Him in order to go to Heaven. They assume that only religious fanatics think like that! Some people will say that having a belief in God is not really necessary, as long as you are kind to people. Whereas others think their belief in a God qualifies them for Heaven, as long as they don't molest young children or murder anyone, of course.

Because ordinary folks don't do these horrible things, they assume they live good lives. In fact, most people you meet on the street in

Australia would be extremely offended if you called them a sinner and said that they were heading for Hell! Australians believe that Jesus Christ was a very good person who did good works and helped people who were poor and needy. Some people may even say that Jesus Christ died on the Cross and He was the Son of God! But they don't believe that they have to change their life in any way, in order to please God. They will confidently say that God will accept them because He knows their good heart intentions!

Because of people's ignorance in these matters, I strongly believe that I have to build solid relationships with those around me in order to give them the option to ask me certain questions such as: "What is it about you? Why do you go to church? Why do you focus so much on Jesus?" When they actually come forth with just one of those questions, I immediately know that the Holy Spirit is preparing their heart for salvation!

If you have tried to answer questions about the Bible from what someone told you, or what you have learnt to say, then there is a better way. I believe that the best way to answer people's questions is from your heart, not your head! Also, I have found that one of the best things I can say to a person who's seeking an answer to a difficult question is: "I'll need to check with my pastor. I'm not going to try to give you an answer that I am not totally sure about myself."

Telling people that you don't understand or haven't got an answer is one of the more honest and effective things that you can do. This book isn't going to cover material that I don't understand, or things I have not experienced. It's only going to cover things that I understand.

Some people who operate in Prophetic Evangelism minister the gift of healing to people and actually heal strangers in the streets. I hope one day that I will be able to do that, but I'm not moving in the gift of healing at the moment. I've been used by God to heal a couple of people, but I'm not effectively walking in that gift at the moment, so I can't teach it. It would be a better book if I could teach on healing, but I'm not personally walking in it at the moment.

People understand and accept you for who you are! Your everyday life at home, at work, or in public places, *is to bring glory to God and that is my definition of evangelism!* It's not the words you say about Jesus, or about your faith, it's the way that you treat others that's really noticed. It's the way that you go ahead with your life despite the circumstances, or the pains and the troubles in the world. It's the way that you unconsciously conduct yourself.

In much the same way as you can always tell a confident person by the way they dress, speak and conduct themselves. Conversely, you can mostly tell if someone is down on their luck or homeless, by the way they dress and by the way they hold themselves.

People are looking at the way you hold yourself. For example: a person's confident stride says: "Don't mess with me, I'm in a hurry! But if a person has a lost or worried expression, they are open to a short friendly greeting. There are people who are really looking for genuine humility in others and also they're looking for love, compassion and understanding. Some people are looking for help and for answers in life, yet the world to them, seems to have passed them by.

Therefore, know that Jesus wants you to develop these attributes: humility, love, compassion and understanding. In fact, He wants you to develop all the fruit of the Holy Spirit in your life, so you can be more sensitive to the needs of others and be an effective evangelist. Realize that you can be more effective in demonstrating God's Kingdom to people that you already know right now.

Evangelism includes sharing your testimony with others. By that, I don't mean for you to say: "Well, once I was lost and once I didn't know Jesus. Then I became a Christian and now my life is a whole lot different!" I think it's far better if you can simply share your ongoing testimonies in small parts as the circumstances dictate. I will give you an example:

My unsaved friend noticed that I was not myself one day, so I told him the truth: I shared with him that: "my older brother, whom I have highly honored and adored all my life, had recently been committed to a psychiatric ward for treatment." I was feeling sad only because of him.

I went on to share: "but a few years ago, God gave me a prophecy about my brother's future. That prophecy warned that Satan was going to try and take my brother out - big time! Everyone would think that his business success was gone forever. But God was going to turn everything around and my brother would be more successful than ever before."

I continued: "My brother has a great future, so I just have to go on thanking God that He is the One in control! God is *always* true to His word! I need to dwell on the fact that one day, my brother *will come out* of his terrible depression and *he will be* very successful and happy."

If my friend had been an unbeliever, I could have gone on to say that Jesus says in the book of Revelation that He's the Alpha and the Omega – the First and the Last and He is everything in between. I could have shared with him that Jesus knew my brother before he was even born. Jesus knew his future and He does have a good plan for him. Deep in my heart, I do have God's peace. I know that regardless of the present circumstances and no matter how out of control he is at the moment, that God's plan for his life will be fulfilled in every detail in God's perfect timing. Sometimes, I just feel a bit sad, that's all.

Sharing a personal story, such as that with someone is a way of sharing your testimony. It's a way of sharing the good news of Jesus Christ. Essentially, you just have to present Jesus Christ as a living reality in your own life. *No one can dispute a personal testimony!*

So if people in your workplace are struggling with a boss who is really aggressive, know that your actions toward your boss will be noticed. Your actions around other staff members, by not gossiping and complaining, stand out like a sore thumb. For example: if you hurt your thumb and it's really sore, then you are constantly aware of it. Every time you use your hand, it really hurts.

What I am saying is: to be an effective evangelist around the people you interact with, you have to stand out like that sore thumb! Even in negative situations, your attitude and your reactions have to be different to those around you and they will quietly observe that difference!

They may not come and say: "Why do you react differently to us?" It's great if they do comment, but know that we are all on a journey. Just know that your life and interaction with people may only be a "seed" in their life. Trust God to nourish that seed.

These people may later on have more questions about God and His Holy Spirit; they may even ask someone else who's a Christian, but they'll always remember you as a Christian they admired. They'll always remember that your life continually demonstrated your faith in God. Perhaps, one day, when they are experiencing a deep personal need, they will call out to God in desperation and humility and He will respond to their prayer of faith.

Please remember, as we've covered before, that the Holy Spirit is smart! We just need to do our part by shining our light. We need to share the Good News of Jesus through our actions and through what we do - rather than with words. So many people are quick to speak words and feel that they've done their duty, by telling people that they're going to hell unless they repent!

These people honestly believe they've done their duty, but they've offended and hurt a person. Yet, they have all sorts of excuses, why that's the right thing to do. They may complain of being rejected, but they believe that they have shared the Gospel and that person has been given a chance to repent. But in reality, no one is actually given a chance if they've been pressured into a decision by a god that would send them to hell. (God doesn't *want* any human being in Hell!)

People need to experience the love of God in their life; this could start with you demonstrating it. They need to know that you accept them for who they are, rather than judging them for who they are! People will see for themselves, the love of Christ flowing through you. They will secretly want what you have. They want to find a person who loves them despite all their flaws and slowly, they'll start to open up and share with you, that their own life is not going well and is in fact coming undone.

It's in those situations, that you speak to them the words that you feel the Holy Spirit is giving you, to comfort them. Don't move in and pounce on that situation by saying, "You need to become a Christian," but simply say, "Can I pray for you? Do you mind if I take your issues before God next time I'm praying in my home, or would you rather I pray for you here in person, that your situation would be resolved?"

People are very open to Christians praying for them. Know that you can have a powerful effect on a person when you pray. They will remember the prayer, especially when it is answered! God will use every opportunity He can to reach a person. Often, He brings people to the end of their rope, just so they'll ask someone they trust for help. So be aware that the Holy Spirit is moving and that He wants to, moment by moment, guide you to others.

An evangelist is essentially being a Christ-like person! You don't have to win a hundred souls to God, to be an effective evangelist! Someone else might win your friend to Jesus one day, but you can be sure that your influence and the seeds you planted in faith were the major reasons why they became a Christian. You prepared their life to be a good soil for the Gospel to be shared in.

In conclusion: Let me say here. It's awesome to share the Gospel with a friend or work colleague and win them to Jesus! It's just that people these days desperately need to know that you love them for who they are, before you try and change them.

eight

What is Prophetic Evangelism?

One of the typical examples of Prophetic Evangelism in the Gospels was when Jesus approached the woman at the well in Samaria. He first asked her for a cup of water and later He said, "Can you bring your husband here?"

And she said, "I have no husband."

He responded, "You've spoken correctly. In fact, you have no husband. You've had five husbands beforehand and the guy you're living with at the moment isn't your husband."

That's an example of Prophetic Evangelism. It is the ability to speak a word of prophecy from God to a total stranger.

The example above happened over 2,000 years ago. Now, what is Prophetic Evangelism today?

It's still the same thing! It's using one of the three gifts of prophecy in a situation with a total stranger. The vast majority of the strangers that I approach would be non-Christians. I know this to be true because of the content of the prophetic word I am given for them. When I give a word to a believer, Christian terminology comes out of my mouth and I'm able to assess that I'm talking to a fellow-believer.

However, most of the Prophetic Evangelism that I do here in Australia is for non-Christians. The fact that only five percent of Australians go to church would most likely account for this. If you are from the United States, perhaps, your national church attendee rate is higher than ours.

A person, of course, doesn't necessarily have to be a non-Christian for you to be doing Prophetic Evangelism. As a Christian myself, I can assure you that it's wonderful, when out of the blue, I am approached by someone with a word from God for me. Prophecy is a tremendous gift and it's something really beautiful for *anyone* to receive from a total stranger. Because of my videos and writings, people at times write to me on the internet, to just encourage me or to give me a prophetic word. I'm always blown away by their kindness.

I love Prophetic Evangelism because it allows me to take a special word of God to a total stranger. Always be assured that God will show you who to speak to, but we'll deal with that in another chapter. I love the fact, that Prophetic Evangelism opens the eyes of a total stranger, with the reality that God knows and cares for them, by actively taking an interest in their life.

With most strangers that I encounter, the Lord uses a gift called the Word of Knowledge. This is knowledge of a particular person about their past or present. It's information that you'd not ordinarily know. Jesus used this gift when He spoke to the woman in Samaria, to say that she was living with someone who she wasn't married to and she'd had specifically five husbands in the past.

The prophetic word that Jesus used in that instance, brought up questions from the woman, which led to further discussion. Just fifty years ago in Australia, it would have caused shame for a woman to have a baby without being married. Only the sexually "liberated" woman openly lived with a non-spouse, or had children outside of marriage. These children were known as the "flower" children. Their parents often gloried in the fact that they were "out on the edge" sort of people who lived as they pleased, without the crushing rules of society!

I do admire the fact that they had the ability to live outside the expected norm and it obviously sat okay with them. They rejected mainstream religion and its rules being enforced on them. They lived aside all that! Unlike a hypocrite, they dared to be different and I respect that.

However, at the time when Jesus spoke to the Samaritan woman, it would have been an extremely shameful thing for a woman to be living with a partner. Even just fifty years ago, it was shameful. Two thousand years ago, it must have been unheard of!

Jesus in a friendly, but very penetrating way, silently put His finger on that situation in her life to say, "I know more about you than meets the eye. I know this about you and this brings you much shame, I believe." He didn't say that exactly, but that's what was implied in what He was doing. So when the Lord sends you out with a prophetic word for a stranger, He normally wants to pinpoint something or say something that will especially affect the person.

Not every time that I give a prophetic word to a stranger, do I first tell them that I'm a Christian and that the prophetic word comes from God. At these times, *after* giving them a word, I'll say: "You may think that I am a clairvoyant but I'm not. I'm a prophet of God and that message was directly from Him. So you can take stock in it and believe in it, because God means what He says, so my words today from Him are going to come true."

The typical prophetic word that I give to a stranger, most often starts with a Word of Knowledge (i.e. Information about them that I wouldn't normally know.) Then the prophecy may move on with a Word of Wisdom, which is a directional word, or what to do with the information that I've just given them, or God's solution for them at the right time.

For example, I was going through a suburb and I passed a guy, and the Lord said, "Go back and give him a prophetic word."

I went back and I said, "Excuse me. I have a gift and from time-to-time, I receive a message for a person, and today I have one for you. Can I share it?" And he defiantly said, "No!"

Ninety-nine percent of the time my normal approach works, but from time-to-time, I get a "No!"

I said, "Ah, listen to me. I'm not here to preach to you! I'm here to give you a special message. I have a real gift and God has a personal message - just for you! I really think you'd benefit from hearing it." I looked at the girl sitting with him and I said, "You'd like to hear it, wouldn't you?" And she nodded her head, so he relented and I could tell him my message.

I remember that I said to him that he was someone who looks for opportunities and a person who's keen to further himself in life. I said that within the next six months, an opportunity was coming along and his friends would say to him that the opportunity was too good to be true. Perhaps something like he's going to open a business with no money down. His friends and family are going to be saying it's too good to be true, but you'll remember this prophetic word because your friend here will remind you of it.

You'll take the opportunity and you will have great success! People will look at your success and say that you had a lucky break.

But I want you to know, that when this business opportunity comes your way, your friend here will remember our conversation today. She will tell you to take up the offer, because it's the one the stranger on the street told you about. She will encourage you and say that it's not too good to be true. It will work out great!

The fact is, "Yes, it was a lucky break, but you took the risk in taking up the opportunity. You'll owe it to the fact that your girlfriend remembered our conversation today. So I hope you're blessed and I hope that you'll take up that opportunity when it presents itself in the next six months. God Bless." I said good-bye to him and walked down the street.

That was a prophetic word. That's an example of something that Satan doesn't want to happen. On two accounts, Satan didn't want that to happen. Satan doesn't want people to be successful in life and he doesn't want them to follow God's advice.

Without that prophetic word, he probably would have listened to his friends and his family and he would have missed out on God's plan for his life. In taking up the offer, God will receive all the glory: forever when he's successful, he'll remember that it was God who actually set up the opportunity for him. As I've said beforehand, the Holy Spirit is pretty big and the Holy Spirit is pretty smart. He knows how to win glory for God and remind a person of a prophetic word.

It's not our job to convert everyone to whom we give a prophetic word. It's our job to be obedient and deliver what the Lord has given to us. I hope I have adequately described what a prophetic word is and what Prophetic Evangelism is.

nine

Can All People Do It?

Can all people do Prophetic Evangelism? More importantly, is it possible that *you* could do it? Yes, it is. The only requirement you need is the ability to hear from God and later in this book, you will find a prayer of impartation of the gift of prophecy. Open your spiritual ears, so you can hear what God is saying. Later on, I will give you an opportunity to prophesy over me.

I encourage you to prophesy over friends and family and people in your church so you gain confidence in the gift. Then, it's just a matter of listening to the Holy Spirit and stepping out to speak to strangers. I have been fortunate to have a few friends who have taken my lead and been encouraged by me, to step out with me and personally witness to strangers on the street, through Prophetic Evangelism.

All my friends know that I'm a Prophetic Evangelist. You could say that I've imparted a little of my calling onto my prophetic friends. I believe prophecy is totally possible for any Christian, who has a relationship with Jesus Christ and wants to bring a message to the world.

I think the number-one attribute that would qualify you to walk in Prophetic Evangelism is the ability to love people! Having the capacity to love all people, including the lost and total strangers, is the number-one attribute needed to walk in Prophetic Evangelism.

Sharing a prophetic word could put people on a detour toward God. You could essentially be rescuing people from the jaws of hell. The fact that you are not expected to convert people takes the pressure off. You simply have to deliver the particular message that Jesus has for you to give.

For instance, think about when a new theology or teaching was first presented to you, or perhaps, when a certain verse in the Bible was explained in a fresh way. Most people do not readily accept new information. Sometimes it takes much research and prayer on our part to accept new concepts and to incorporate them into our own life! So too, your prophetic word may just be a stepping-stone for a non-Christian to come closer to discovering the reality of Jesus Christ.

You can be sure that nearly every person whom you give a prophetic word to, will have someone, perhaps a close friend, a parent, a relative, or even a neighbor praying for them! Someone will have been already praying for their salvation and you, coming alongside them and giving them a prophetic word, is an answer to that prayer. Bear in mind that all you need to have is the Holy Spirit to lead you and His love in your heart for people.

So many times, I find it's really scary to give a prophetic word to a total stranger. There's a sense of trepidation, especially when you have to walk up to someone and sort of interrupt their conversation. Not only do you have to present your word to the right person, but you also know that the person with them will be listening to you! It takes holy boldness and strength of character to do that, but that strength of character and that holy boldness comes from the love that you have and the compassion that you have for others. This itself, I believe, is a gift from God.

Truly, love conquers all fear. Love breaks through all the fear of man and it also combats Satan's onslaughts. Love breaks through all fear that would stop you from giving a prophetic word. Love really is the supreme act of kindness. The supreme act of love is of course, to give your life for another. However, I truly believe that walking up to a total stranger and giving them a message of hope directly from God's heart to them is a wonderful way to express Christian love.

What qualifies you? Can all people do it? Yes! Even you can do it.

All it takes is love and compassion for the broken hearted. Do you love people? Do you have a natural tendency to love people, or are you someone who really doesn't care about others? Do you have an honest desire to evangelize people and bring them into the kingdom?

The fact that you are reading this book proves that you already have a keen interest in evangelizing people through the prophetic word. You wouldn't read so many pages into a book if you didn't have a keen love for people and an earnest desire to reach them through Prophetic Evangelism.

I believe you're more than qualified! But it's not the number of pages that you read in this book that will qualify you. It's not the number of hours that you spend in prayer that will qualify you. It's not the amount of Bible passages that you can quote that will qualify you. What qualifies you to be a Prophetic Evangelist is your ability to love people. Love truly is the number-one requirement for you to launch out and do Prophetic Evangelism with any success.

ten

Does God Want Me?

Not long before Jesus left the earth and ascended in a cloud to Heaven, He had instructed His disciples to "go out into the world and preach the Gospel and make disciples of all men." That was two thousand years ago, but today, as His disciples, it's our instruction. To become a disciple, you must respond to the Gospel. To respond, you must understand it, to understand, the Holy Spirit works in you. For this to happen, a spiritual "seed" needs to be sown in your heart by someone – that someone could be you giving a prophetic word!

Salvation, therefore, is a long process even though in reality, it appears to be instant! Many believers are not versed in sharing the Gospel. Fear of man stops others! Many believers feel "stuck"- they seem paralyzed and feel that they don't have the capacity within themselves to share the message of hope with people who are living and dying around them. Know that God uses any willing believer to plant a tiny "seed" that will lead to salvation, eventually!

Does God want you? Yes, He's called you! Therefore, he wants you. The fact you're reading this book proves you have an interest in God's commission.

You know that you already have an interest in this subject. It's something close to your heart. Can He use you? Yes, He can! He can use any Christian who is open to the Holy Spirit. In fact, when you start to move in prophecy and into Prophetic Evangelism, you'll find that your relationship with God will drastically improve: your relationship with Jesus and the Father will become far more intimate, as you hear and see messages that they have for other people.

These messages come from God's heart to His people. As you hear God's heart and as you hear messages come out of your mouth for others, you'll just fall more and more in love with Jesus. You'll fall more and more in love with the Father as you see your messages from Him helping lost and dying souls.

It's an encouraging thing to walk up to strangers and give them a message about their current life and the life that God wants them to lead. In one dimension of their life, you give them a message that will help improve and prosper them. God is clearly able to show you that He loves all people. He's clearly able to show you more dimensions of His heart, as you go out and share His message with those that He calls you to go to. Often, God will have a personal message for you that He'll put in your heart, to share with another person.

Many times, there will be a message that God wants you personally to hear, but you speak it to another person. You'll find that as you speak it to the other person, that it's speaking really loudly to yourself. Sometimes, we're not really receptive to messages from God. Sometimes, we close ourselves to hearing from God. Often, He'll use a prophetic word to someone else, to speak deeply to you. The prophetic word is like a two-pronged instrument. It touches the person for whom it's meant, but it can also touch you.

I was part of a prophetic group on Facebook and we gave prophecies to strangers and all the prophecies were posted on the main wall. People who came to the website could read the prophecies for others on the main wall. Not only was the person given the prophecy edified, but we discovered that many people who visited the wall, actually found parts in the prophecies that applied to them as well.

Please be assured that the gift of prophecy is something that God wants you to be involved in. God yearns to move you from just being a spectator, into a participator. He wants to raise thousands and thousands of people, to move in Prophetic Evangelism and to take the Gospel supernaturally out into the streets. He has a vested interest in employing you. You don't have to come with lots of qualifications. It's not an assignment. There's not a list of examinations you need to pass to be a Prophetic Evangelist. There is no set course!

There's no certificate or degree that you have to complete, to become one of the most effective evangelists in the world. All it takes is a little practice and courage, but first and foremost, as I've mentioned before, it takes the capacity to love strangers. You have to have within yourself, a capacity and a desire to set the captives free and break open the chains that are binding people. If you have these attributes, then God wants you.

God is going to use you and take you out into the world and make you an effective Prophetic Evangelist. There is no measurement scale. There is no scale that says that you're better than me or I'm better than you. The Lord has specific messages that He wants given to each person walking down the street that He calls us to. I'm pretty sure that if He gave you a message for a stranger, that He'd give me the exact same message and we'd both deliver it similarly and the same effect would be had with the person.

It's not as though I'm more skilled, or I have more ability than you. I believe that the prophetic gift in you would be able to communicate the message just as clearly as I could. There aren't many excuses why you wouldn't move ahead and not take it on. I just know that Jesus loves you and He wants to use you. You may have fears, but fear is a natural thing! Know that fear is something we often have before we have a breakthrough.

Fear creates a sort of boundary for us and it's a sort of thing that keeps us in check, keeps us safe. It's natural to have fears! It's natural for you to have a little fear in you about this whole subject. I know certainly that the enemy doesn't want you moving out in this gift. He doesn't want God setting you loose on hundreds of souls and for them to change. But God wants you to do it and being a child of God makes you qualified. He's called you to do it. He wants you to do it. Just put your hand up and say, "Yes, Lord, use me!"

eleven

The Gift of Prophecy

Paul encourages us in Corinthians to desire the best gifts. He encourages us to desire and even covet the gift of prophecy. It says also that the best gift is prophecy.

The Apostle told us that all believers should prophesy and all of us should desire to prophesy. Prophecy is a tremendous gift. It's something that not only blesses the person who receives the prophecy, but it also blesses the person who is giving it. It's a tremendous and wonderful thing to do. It's exciting to walk down the street and find a person who the Lord wants you to give a prophecy to.

I remember some time ago, I was walking down the street and I saw the favor of God on a woman. I said to her, "I see success and favor on your life and that this year, you're going to have some sort of promotion or some sort of success come into your life. It's radiating on you and it's about to happen. So, God Bless You."

She was surprised, but happy and her boyfriend with her was happy too. It's tremendous to confidently be able to share with a person that something good was going to happen in their life. When that promotion or success comes, God will be glorified, because she will realize that God had blessed her like the stranger had said.

What is prophecy? Many people presume that prophecy is some kind of mystical experience, but prophecy is actually a distinct gift from God. Like all good things from God, the devil has a counterfeit "gift" called clairvoyance. That's why, if I am led to, I set the record straight with certain strangers and make sure that they know that my message to them was from God and that I am not a clairvoyant.

The gift of prophecy is one of three gifts that are used when someone delivers a prophecy. To best explain the gift of prophecy, we need to understand a little about what the other two gifts of prophecy entail. First, we have the gift of the Word of Knowledge. This gift is supernatural information about a person that normally, you couldn't possibly know about their past or present. That is, for instance, when Jesus said to the woman at the well that, "You've had five husbands and the man you're currently living with is not your husband."

When Jesus said that, He was saying a Word of Knowledge – something that takes people by surprise and really shocks them. He said to Nathanial, "You're a man of no guile and I saw you under the tree when you were praying." That was also a Word of Knowledge accompanied by a vision that Jesus saw about Nathanial. When Jesus saw Zacchaeus in the tree and knew his name, this was a Word of Knowledge of Jesus.

Word of Knowledge really makes the hearer take notice! But it is just one of the prophetic gifts.

Another gift of prophecy is the Word of Wisdom, which is a directional word. It's where God has given you directions on something to do with the prophecy. For example: "God's called you to the nations to be a teacher. He wants you to study His word more diligently and spend more time in prayer, because He has a revelation for you in the Word for you to expound on in the future. He wants to show you His mysteries."

Telling the person to spend more time in the Word and in prayer is a Word of Wisdom. It's a directional word. It's something that if they fail to do, they will not be sent to the nations to preach. Therefore, a prophecy's fulfillment depends on being obedient to any words of wisdom contained in it.

The gift of Prophecy is everything in the prophetic message you give, that's not a Word of Wisdom and a Word of Knowledge.

In the sample prophecy I just used, the actual gift of prophecy element, of that prophecy was that "Jesus is going to send him to the nations. Anything that's not a Word of Knowledge and not a Word of Wisdom – that is the gift of prophecy component.

Some people look at the word "prophecy" and assume that prophecy is just about the future. Prophecy can contain things about the future, but it's not necessarily futuristic. God can give a prophecy about someone's present situation and show them how to deal with it or to escape from it. This sort of prophecy is very powerful!

An example of a prophecy containing a Word of Knowledge might be, "You're in a very difficult position at the moment - you've recently lost a loved one. God wants to tell you to hold on and be at peace. He is going to replace that heartache inside you with joy. He's going to bring you comfort and peace and you're going to be in a position that's a whole lot better this time next year."

The Word of Knowledge element was that the person had recently lost someone, then all the comfort being spoken was the gift of prophecy element. There's a Word of Wisdom in there, too. See if you can spot it! (Hold on and be at peace.)

Therefore, one of the best prophecies is made of (1) Word of Wisdom, (2) Word of Knowledge and of course, the actual prophecy element of the prophecy. (That is, everything in the prophecy that doesn't fall into the above two categories)

Most people call everything that comes from a prophet a prophecy. Not many people say that they received a Word of Knowledge and a

Word of Wisdom, but they lump the three separate gifts together and just say that they received a prophecy. That's okay, the Lord doesn't mind that! However, for the purposes of this book, you need to know that most prophecies have one or two of the other components. Prophecies are very encouraging, but as a prophetic evangelist, I often feel that the Word of Knowledge in a prophecy is the most important part because it gets people's attention to listen to the whole prophecy given to them.

Anyone can go and talk about someone's future and not be correct. But you can't go to a person and start sharing Words of Knowledge about them without them immediately knowing it to be true or false. You can't go and share those private snippets of information with them without them acknowledging that you're accurate and this astounds them.

It's actually the Words of Knowledge that are contained in a prophecy that allows a person to remember the prophecy for years and hold faith in the prophecy, because they say to themselves, "He said these things about me and that was amazing, and that much was true. He couldn't possibly have known that." Therefore, they believe that their whole prophecy is going to come true because of the elements of Word of Knowledge.

Prophecies are exciting. That lady who I told that success was coming this year to her was certainly excited. I told her that I was not a clairvoyant, but I'm a prophet and I receive my information from God. I went on to say that when that promotion or that success comes into her life, to take time out and to thank God for it. We both smiled and she said she would do that.

To me that was validation that they believed in the prophecy. So, it's a good thing to believe in your prophecies. It's even better to have them written out and to regularly acknowledge them over your life. Until they are fulfilled, keep them close to your heart.

Prophecy is in the domain of God and God is the One who is sovereign. He allows a prophetic word to come true. I trust that I've explained what prophecy is and I hope you have a better understanding of the particular gift called prophecy.

twelve

The Gift of the Word of Knowledge

As we discussed earlier, a Word of Knowledge is supernatural information about a person that you wouldn't ordinarily know.

When you share a Word of Knowledge, a person really starts to listen intently. You can interrupt a person speaking with friends and say, "Excuse me, I have a gift and from time-to-time that gift allows me to receive a message for a person. Today, I have a message for you. Would you like to hear it?" Most people reply, "Yes" but sometimes, they seem a little skeptical.

When they agree, you can prophesy over them. If God gives you a Word of Knowledge, the skepticism fades fast. I remember once, when I approached a lady in a doctor's surgery and said. "You recently lost your precious cat and you've been grieving ever since. You've been crying many tears because of it. God in Heaven even cries tears for you!

Everyone who knows you, people at work, people at home, your family – all of them know you're grieving. But God wants you to know that the grieving will be over one day. Things will be better and you'll be able to find another cat. Buy another cat to love. So please know that the grieving is going to stop soon and God's going to give you His comfort."

Most of that prophecy was a Word of Knowledge.

Two weeks earlier, the woman had lost her much loved cat and had been suffering grief ever since. That day, in a doctor's surgery in Brisbane, I delivered mostly a Word of Knowledge. Everyone waiting in the surgery stopped talking and had listened to me. From memory, there were three patients and the receptionist who was with the woman that I had walked in to tell.

They were all dumbfounded that I'd walked in and just read the mail of the person who was serving. The lady was very emotional and had begun to cry. She was blessed in knowing that God had sent me into the surgery and that she was going to have peace again. That's an example of a Word of Knowledge.

I had information for a guy once in my taxicab when I used to drive taxis. Jesus asked me to say, "Have you been in touch with your brother lately?

He said, "No, my brother's dead to me."

I said, "That's a shame because at the moment he's on his death-bed. He's dying of cancer and he wants to contact you."

He says, "How do you know that?"

And I said, "Jesus just told me. Apparently your mom won't pass on your phone number because there's bad blood between you. Your brother's a Christian now and he's been praying that God will cause you to contact him, because he wants to make peace with you before he passes on. He wants you to know that he is happy. He has a good relationship with God and he's happy and ready to go to Heaven. He's looking forward to that. But he just wants to say good-bye to you before he goes and make sure everything's okay between you and him, before he dies."

The guy became quite emotional and assured me that he was going to ring his mother when he left my cab. Again, a Word of Knowledge had a deep effect on someone.

Now I will tell you that sharing Words of Knowledge is scary! But as I've said before, they make a prophecy stand up. It makes a prophecy last for many years when you share great Words of Knowledge. There are numerous people going around sharing prophecies, which are nice flowery words, not containing Words of Knowledge in them. I believe that those prophecies are very weak and don't really stand strong. They don't stand the test of time because they don't really impact the person enough for them to remember what you actually said to them.

So, I encourage you to bite the bullet! That's an Australian term. I'm not sure if you understand that in America, but I encourage you to suck in your fear and start to move in the Word of Knowledge. If, or when, God tells you something about another person that you wouldn't ordinarily know - or something about their life or their past, present or future, pass it on.

We're talking about delivering prophecies to strangers, so really your knowledge about them would be extremely limited. In fact, you wouldn't know anything. I encourage you to give those Words of Knowledge. Don't hold them back. Don't just say something that sounds good, but say what the Lord has put on your heart. I can't stress this enough.

I heard a prophecy in my life about twenty-five years ago that talked about my future. It spoke about me being in a very dark tunnel and how I was going to come through a healing process. The man prophesied and said that I would be feeling that there was no light showing in my life. He said that I was going to come out of this dark tunnel one day and go through healing. He said that when I received healing, I would start to minister for God powerfully. What the person said was so accurate! It was amazing.

It's that Word of Knowledge that has kept me believing in the prophecy that one day I'll be fully healed and one day I'll be raised in the ministry and do great things. He said in that prophecy that I was going to make a big difference in the world. I am still looking forward to his good report to manifest in my life.

So I want to encourage you to use the Word of Knowledge. I know I've said it already in this chapter, but it's so essential. The difference between a good prophecy and a weak prophecy are the Words of Knowledge.

There is a famous author and prophet, Rick Joyner, who writes books and shares and preaches around the world. He says that if a stranger writes to his ministry and gives him directional words like Words of Wisdom for him to take an action or a particular course in his ministry - he won't take the course, or he won't take the action, unless the prophecy also contains a substantial amount of Word of Knowledge in it.

Here is a well known and trusted prophet who knows the voice of the Lord and can understand and discern His voice. Yet, he still says that he won't take directions from an unknown prophet if they don't contain the Words of Knowledge.

If Rick Joyner, who is a well-known and respected prophet in the world, is that serious about the Word of Knowledge, so should you be! So should I be! I've become very good at Word of Knowledge myself. It's something that I've practiced and I've spent a lot of time doing. In fact, almost every prophecy I give has a Word of Knowledge or two or three, or even four. I try to lace my prophecies with Words of Knowledge and have as many in there as I can.

I nearly always lead with a Word of Knowledge. They're so important. I can't impress upon you how important they are. Imagine a prophecy as a building going up and as the bricks are laid, the Word of Knowledge is like the mortar or the cement between the bricks. They hold the whole building together. You couldn't put up a brick wall or put up a house without cement on the bricks. You just can't lay the bricks together, they will just fall down.

Likewise, a prophecy without Words of Knowledge will fall to the ground. It won't have the desired effect over the years that it may have had. It simply won't sustain the years without Words of Knowledge in it - these allow a person to hold onto the unknown element spoken about their life through the prophet.

Yes, Words of Knowledge can be risky! If you get it wrong with a person, you have lost your credibility straight away. I'm sure that this is the major reason that people resist openly sharing the Word of Knowledge. They don't want to be seen as a false prophet! However, I believe that the real reason for not sharing is unbelief in God's goodness, or pride or embarrassment! You must search your own heart and seek the Holy Spirit's help to overcome any negative thoughts that Satan thrusts into your mind.

In reality, just know that if you're going to operate in prophecy, you need to operate like God wants you to. I can assure you that God loves the Word of Knowledge because He knows how powerful it is.

So, I encourage you with all my heart to step out and boldly speak out any Words of Knowledge that God gives you.

thirteen

The Gift of the Word of Wisdom

As we've discussed in Chapter 11, Words of Wisdom are directional words of God. I will use an example of this recorded in the Old Testament. One time in Israel's history, the King was told by his appointed prophet to: *go out at night and dig a series of trenches.* Elisha, the prophet of God, said that there would be no wind or rain, but the ditches would fill with water and there would be enough water to satisfy both the army and all their animals. It seemed a strange request, but it was a Word of Wisdom of God through the mouth of His prophet, on how to win the war!

So the King instructed his generals to do exactly what the prophet of God said, that is, to carry out the Word of Wisdom. The army went out and prepared to face their enemy. They went and dug a whole lot of trenches and waited on the Lord. The next day, when the water was in the trenches, the enemy looked down and wrongly assumed that the trenches were filled with blood and there appeared to be blood all over the ground. Was their enemy already dead?

Because of what they saw, the enemy army came down for a closer look and when they did, the Israeli army ambushed them! You see, the Word of Wisdom had also said to mount an ambush, *"They'll come down and you're to ambush them when they came down."* So that's exactly what happened. (This historical event is recorded in 2 Kings Chapter 3)

In ancient Israel, a king would always go to a prophet of God, or call a prophet before him and ask him for directions, or to seek answers to their questions. The king would not only ask for directions concerning his armies, but he would seek his prophet's directions concerning all important matters relating to the house of Israel. Today, all over the world, God still has his prophets, but unfortunately, most of our leaders would not seek godly advice from them.

However, today, God still has specific directions that He has for all people. He wants us to follow His directions because He loves us all and wants the very best for us, at all times. It would be ideal if everyone heard from the Lord. Certainly in the parable of the Good Shepherd, Jesus taught that we are all like sheep that need a shepherd. He said that He IS the Good Shepherd.

As His sheep, we are supposed to be able to hear our Good Shepherd's voice! Yet, this is not true today. Many Christians confess that they have never heard God's voice. (Perhaps they are assuming God's voice will boom out loud and therefore they ignore His quiet voice in their spirit.) God also wants His sheep to follow His directions. Wouldn't it be tremendous if the entire worldwide church of God heard and obeyed their Good Shepherd?

The prophet of God instructed Israel on the way to go and the way to act. The people holding the highest authority at the time were the Prophet of God, the High Priest and Israel's King. These three important people had exceptional power over the common people.

Today, our Risen Lord Jesus Christ totally fulfills each of those roles.

Therefore, wouldn't it be wonderful if everyone who claims to belong to Jesus would actually do the things that He says! Sadly, that's not happening and the world suffers. I am totally convinced that God wants more and more of His people to be raised up in the prophetic ministry. By speaking out His words to people, they will better know the love of God and how to best live their personal life on this wonderful planet called Earth.

Therefore, as you go out, prepared to do Prophetic Evangelism, be confident that God has specific directions for people to receive. Whether they're a Christian or not, God wants everyone to know that He loves them and He's interested in making their life successful. However, to follow His directions, they need to know them! God has the best answer to any situation and He may just use you to deliver His answer to a stranger.

Often, when I give a prophetic word to a stranger, I start with Words of Knowledge about the person's situation and I often end with me giving Words of Wisdom or directions to the person on how to handle that situation. This will be the best way how to deal with that situation or how to face a future situation. One of the directions I gave to a couple recently was to give praise to God when a particular success happens. That was a Word of Wisdom.

They were to give God the honor for this coming success. God's way is perfect – it's always the best way! Sometimes, we assume that our way is better, but if we receive God's directions, we've received a perfect way that will work out one hundred percent.

As a Prophetic Evangelist, you'll be approaching people and telling them simple directions on how to handle things, or how to take positive future steps according to what God wants them to do. It'll be in a simple message and it's really easy to share, but it'll be an integral thing for them to do. It'll qualify whether or not they're going to be successful in the venture that they have, or will have, in their present or future life.

Just as Word of Knowledge and Word of Wisdom are important to share with people, it wouldn't be a good thing for you to hear in your mind or in your heart, God's words and then, fail to deliver them. Word of Wisdom is particularly important. The fulfillment of a prophecy depends on every Word of Wisdom being fully adhered to by the hearer: to fail in this matter, the prophecy is automatically nullified.

You may in fact be holding up someone's life by sharing a prophecy and leaving out the particular Word of Wisdom that the Lord has for them! It's therefore vital to deliver every Word of Wisdom God gives you. Even if they sound a little silly or strange to you, speak them out!

I vividly remember one time when I gave a famous preacher about ten minutes of Words of Wisdom. I suggested he publish a book because God was giving me the names of one subject after another on the things that he was to address. Some of the subject names surprised me somewhat, but I repeated them as God said them to me.

This particular man is a remarkable preacher. He has preached to hundreds of thousands of people and has caused multitudes to come to know the Savior. It was a remarkable prophecy and I felt extremely honored to pass on to him exactly what God was telling him to do. It really did take a lot of confidence and faith for me to prepare the video for him and send it to him, but I knew that God wanted him to hear it.

Part of me wanted to shrink back and not deliver that prophecy to him, because it contained so many directions from God. Who am I? I'm just a simple unknown man with a camera and a yearning to be used by God. Why would he take notice of something from a total stranger?

However, I received a message back from his secretary to say that he'd watched the video and that he would be applying all the directions that God had said in the prophecy. By this, he showed himself to be a very humble man of God. I was pleased that God's Word had hit its mark and that he was going to obey the Words of Wisdom in the prophecy.

Sometimes, with a stranger, it might be an important businessman, or if you're a guy, it might be a lady who is very attractive. Just know that all fear on your part must be overcome. Maybe, you spot a guy stepping out of the driver's seat of a shiny BMW and God gives you a word, just respond to it! Regardless of your initial judgment about someone, you are not to be so intimidated that you fail to pass on a specific Word of Wisdom to a person.

Just trust that the Lord has anointed your voice and He is going to carry through your prophecy with His anointing and His power. Just trust that He'll give you the boldness to deliver the Word of Wisdom to the person who seems to be intimidating you somehow with their presence, or how they're holding themselves. It's important to deliver the words of Wisdom, because as I've said, the success of a certain aspect of someone's life will depend on following God's advice.

I hope that you've been blessed by this. I trust that you now understand what a Word of Wisdom is. May you have much success in delivering God's Words of Wisdom to others!

fourteen

Bringing Them All Together

We have at this stage discussed prophecy, Word of Knowledge and Word of Wisdom. I now want to bring all of those elements together in a prophecy and deliver it to a person in a way that they can understand and remember.

The example I will use to illustrate this is the story I have already used. It's the story where I shared with a man in my taxi that *his brother was dying of cancer.* (That was a Word of Knowledge.) *His brother wanted to contact him, but his mother had said "No."* (This too, was a Word of Knowledge.) The part about *his sick brother wanting to make peace* (was part Word of Knowledge and part prophecy.)

My words to my passenger: *"You should get in contact with your brother because he wants to make peace with you before he dies,"* (This was a Word of Wisdom followed by a Word of Knowledge) *"And your brother loves you and wants to make peace with you"* (was also a Word of Knowledge,) while, *"before he dies,"* (was prophecy.)

God's message to him through me that day resulted in a passenger of mine becoming very emotional and promising that he was going to first contact his mother and then contact his brother. He asked me if he has enough time to contact his brother, before his brother died and I said, "Yes, you will have time if you'd make the effort to phone your mother."

Not every prophecy that you deliver may have every element of the prophetic gift in it, but it's handy if they do have at least two elements of prophecy in it. However, a really great prophecy will contain the whole three elements - it's very substantial and beneficial to the hearer.

It's important to be aware that there's a limit to what the average person is able to handle or to remember when you deliver a prophetic word. You must always be mindful of that!

Therefore, say only what the Holy Spirit leads you to say. He never gets it wrong! Too much information can easily frustrate and worry people. They could be trying so hard to listen to you speaking that they forget everything you tell them! I've been in that position myself, when listening to someone prophesying over me. Be assured, the Holy Spirit does already know exactly what they can handle. He is very smart, you know!

If you are like me, you would love to hear someone gifted in prophecy to pepper their message with Word of Knowledge. Why? This is because Word of Knowledge validates the accuracy of a prophetic gift: Word of Knowledge reassures us to believe what is said about our future.

Word of Knowledge directed to me by someone will be about things that I already know, so I don't have to remember these things. But I love the Word of Knowledge because it alone, uniquely provides me the evidence that I am in fact, hearing God's words and that is the thing that constantly thrills me and grabs my full attention.

Always be aware, however, that there is spiritual opposition! Satan has his own way of operating in the supernatural. Clairvoyants can also deliver their own prophetic word to people! They, too, can hear from a supernatural source! The information they give you may seem somewhat accurate, but realize that it comes from a wrong spirit! Mediums

give you information about your life: they can even give you information about people and circumstances in your past, as well as in your
future. Evil spirits are well aware of what is happening on Earth.

Clairvoyants are very skilled at using their spirit guide or demon to
deliver this sort of information to unsuspecting people. Often, these
mostly innocent people are amazed that the medium or clairvoyant
knows them! They are surprised that the psychic indeed knows all
kinds of information about them!

The invisible spiritual world around us is made up of both God's
angels and the wicked fallen angels of the devil, called demons, who
want to deceive us and set us on the wrong path.

I am very serious, be warned, know that once you dabble with
a wrong spirit, it will want more and more control over you! This
supernatural knowledge that comes from the kingdom of darkness
will strongly compel a person to go back time and time again. This
is Satan's intention! He wants people to rely on his demons to satisfy
their spiritual hunger, so that people will not rely on God. Satan knows
that his accurate words to people assist to validate his message to them.

Having said all that, let's revert back to God's words.

Once you've established yourself through Word of Knowledge as
being a supernatural voice in the person's life - then it's time to move
on to the Word of Wisdom, by passing on God's directions for the person to take aboard. Perhaps, if God leads, you can give a future prophecy to them. It's interesting to share things about a person's future, but
it's not essential - God doesn't always give you such a prophetic word.

Most people just need confidence and encouragement about
what's happening in their life at present.

Not every person to whom I give a prophecy, do I talk about their
future. In fact, I'd say only twenty percent of the prophecies I give to
people talk about their future. Also, most prophecies I delivered to a

group that I used to run, spoke about a person's life where it was currently at: and it spoke about what God wanted at that time, for them to know.

God is very interested in every one of us! He's always interested in every stage of our life. Just recognize that it's mostly how we live our life today that is going to affect our future! Therefore, God is very interested in us getting our steps right today, so that our steps will have a good impact on our future and give us a much better future. However, God doesn't always actually talk about our future!

It's also important for us to realize that anyone can talk about the supposed future of a person!

However, the hearer of such a word has no way of knowing if the supposed prophecy is going to come true. But, when you talk about a person's *current* life and what they are to do in their *current situation*, this type of information is far more usable for people.

The three gifts of prophecy are all very important gifts, and they are all well suited to flow together. With time and experience, you will find yourself giving people very comprehensive and valuable prophecies.

I know I go on and on about Words of Knowledge and that's because I suppose I feel they are so important to the credibility and memory retention.

However, each of the three gifts of prophecy was created by God to encourage and edify people, no matter if they are Christians or whether they are people who are not yet saved. If you can recall my words in the early chapters of this book, you will know that I believe every word of prophecy that is spoken to a person is a "seed" planted by God in their soul area that will ultimately help lead them to salvation. That is my number one reason for loving all three of the prophetic gifts.

fifteen

My Favorite Prophecy

You could probably guess from what I've covered so far in the 14 chapters of this book that I love to give a prophecy to people, which contains many Words of Knowledge in it. This type of prophecy quickly establishes to me that the prophecy is coming from God and not from my own mind or emotions. I am particularly thankful for this gift, when God has directed me to approach a pretty girl, and then He gives me a Word of Knowledge for her. I certainly don't want her to think that I have ulterior motives for approaching her.

I know that God loves me, but many unbelievers don't always have that assurance. Words of Knowledge will therefore amaze them. These people are blown away by the fact that God would actually use a total stranger to bring His message to them. Word of Knowledge actually proves to the person that God is really interested in their life and He wants the best for them.

At the risk of appearing ungrateful, when I receive a prophecy from someone and it doesn't have Word of Knowledge in it, I will not bother to keep it. This is because I don't like receiving "flowery" words from people. I want to both give and to receive prophecies that have some kind of substance in them.

I consider myself pretty good at taking directions from God. Therefore, I love to receive a prophecy that has Word of Wisdom on it. I know that if I do my part and follow the Word of Wisdom, then in due time, God will do His part and fulfill the whole prophecy. I certainly love to have copies of these particular prophecies, so that I can go on boldly claiming them until they come to pass. If the devil tries to heap condemnation on me, I might use such prophecies against him. I consider them to be God's spiritual weapons for me to use in time of need.

Along with Word of Knowledge and Word of Wisdom, I love to receive a prophecy that has elements of the future in it. This is not essential, but most times, when the Lord talks about my future, He's actually reminding me of His previous prophecies. Therefore, I see such words as confirmation that the prophecy is from Him. I never tire of hearing about the good things God has in store for me. I'm sure that repeating future prophecies is God's way of helping me to persevere in doing what He wants me to do now! He is very smart! He knows just when I need to be encouraged.

I consider that I have a good and close relationship with the Lord, yet Satan still bombards me with doubts about my future. Even though I have had really big prophecies over my future, I still often get discouraged within myself and think that doors are never going to open up for me. Therefore, God knows that I need to have confirmation of His plans for me, again and again.

God has promised to fulfill my desires and He knows that my desire is to be a travelling preacher and Prophetic-Evangelist. My most earnest desire is for the Holy Spirit to rise up an army of Christians to be able to hear from God. I want to be able to go from church to church and to minister to people so as to train others to hear from God. It's good for God to remind me that the doors are going to open and it's all in His timing. He will open the doors and He will send me.

My favorite sort of prophecy has, as I said, a lot of Word of Knowledge in it, along with some Word of Wisdom and prophecy. I like comforting prophecies about the present or future. I just want to continually know that God is pleased with me.

I never tire of Jesus or the Father, saying to me that they love me, in a prophecy. It's an amazing thing to think that just hearing God say that He loves me, deeply affects me, but it's true. I never tire of hearing it. Sometimes, I have been so bound in sin, that just hearing God say He loves me was enough to break open the water gates of my eyes and bring me to tears.

I never cease to be thankful for the unending grace of God. I continually find it awesome that God has always loved me, despite the sin that I was committing in my life. I am so grateful that the devil, once for all time, has been put in his place by the Cross of Jesus and I am forever thankful to the Holy Spirit for personally lifting the burden of my past guilt. Our Savior Jesus Christ is indeed, the burden bearer. He has removed the condemnation of the devil forever!

sixteen

Long or Short Prophecies?

Should we have short or long prophecies? It depends on your audience and the method of the delivery that you give a prophecy, whether you make a long or short one for someone. If you have a feeling that it could be a long prophecy, you could ask them if they have a phone or any recording device. If they do, then it doesn't matter how long a recorded prophecy is, because it can be replayed whenever they want to hear it. There have been times that I have recorded long five to ten-minute prophecies on peoples' phones. They are blessed to be able to play it repeatedly.

When you're giving prophetic words to strangers, remember that it's great to fill a prophecy with many Words of Knowledge. They don't all have to be remembered. The people you witness to will just remember that you knew all about them. But the Word of Wisdom needs to be adhered to. Therefore, it's vital that the person remembers it and does apply it to their life.

As well as obeying the Word of Wisdom, people need to remember the things that you say about their future. I would say short and sweet is the best policy. If you had a business card printed, you could hand the person one and ask them to contact you if they had any questions. Using a business card is a handy way to continue your relationship with a stranger and a way of forever impacting them.

So I'd say short is a good idea. You can ask the person: "Have you any questions?" Be confident that God will supply the answer to their question to you. Doing this allows you to spend more time with the person, without filling their minds up with an overload of prophecy that they won't be able to recall. The answers to their questions are pretty simple to do and it really opens a way to minister to people more effectively without crowding a prophecy.

So in summary, I think it is best to keep your prophecies shorter rather than longer. Unless, of course, you have a recording device handy, then it can be as long as you feel the Lord's leading.

seventeen

Can I Really Do It?

You would have to ask yourself when you've come this far in the book, if you can really do it. Is it possible for me to prophetically evangelize people on the streets? Is it possible for me to just walk down the street, find a person and deliver a prophetic message to them?

I find that most people that I pray for to receive the gift of prophecy – actually do receive it. I believe that when people ask me for this gift, that their prayer of faith allows them to receive it. Many of them have spoken beautiful words over my life. The first prophecies that they've spoken to me have been very effective and touching. Many of these include the words, "I love you, Matthew and I'm proud of you." They may seem words that are plain to the average person, but I never tire of hearing Jesus say that He loves me.

Is it possible? Can you really do it? That's like asking me whether the Holy Spirit is really part of your life. Is the Holy Spirit in your life? Are you a Christian? Does the Holy Spirit have influence in your life? If the Holy Spirit is in your life, then you can certainly prophesy.

Some people say that the Holy Spirit doesn't speak to them, yet they will openly admit that quite often a thought comes to them to phone someone and then that same person phones them! By that statement, I know that the thought didn't come from their mind in the first place. That was the Holy Spirit speaking to them! We are to always be aware of things like this and be sure to give God the glory.

The Holy Spirit was moving with them to contact that person. Being aware of His promptings becomes easier the more we practice it! The same is true of prophecy.

Not many people are aware that the Spirit of God and the testimony of Jesus are the Spirit of prophecy as it says in Revelation. They don't understand that Jesus wants us all to prophesy. I believe that it's a lie of Satan that is being propagated by some churches that the Holy Spirit only gives the gift of prophecy to particular people. I believe as I do because the Apostle Paul says he wished that all believers would prophesy.

So can you really do it? Yes, you can! You just need to be encouraged! It's very simple to prophesy to anyone. It's not strange nor is it hard! Neither is prophecy something that you *have* to put on the shelf. It's something that God wants you to do.

There are thousands of people out there who are starving for a either a message, or a fresh touch from Jesus. I can't come to your country and walk down your streets and touch people in your area. I'm not part of your workplace or your church. I'm not part of your life so I can't touch people that you interact with. But you can! This book is about developing that gift in your life.

Is there anything in you that says you can't? Is it this idea that prophecy is only for particular people? If you believe that it's for special people, then that idea can be dispelled by the fact that I can do it! I'm just an ordinary and simple guy yet I'm gifted with prophecy and I can move in it very effectively. Actually, if you really knew the things I know about me, it would prove to you that any Christian can be used by God in this way. God wants all His children to be open to the prophetic.

You may wrongly believe that you're not special enough, or you may think that the gift of prophecy isn't for all believers. The Apostle Paul said *that we should covet the best gifts*; he goes on to say that prophecy *is the best gift.* A lot of the other gifts of the Holy Spirit flow out of the prophetic!

I believe that prophecy opens the supernatural realm, because it's exciting to hear a message from God. It's exciting to walk down the street and see a person to whom God wants to minister and share His love with. It's so exciting to spend time with God, then minister out of that presence of God into the lives of others. Prophecy is both desirable and commendable for you to do and it's something that you can do! Simply buying this book and reading it is a good step. Applying this book and moving out in the gift of prophecy is quite another.

I'm confident that you can receive the gift of prophecy and practice it. Can you really do it? Yes, you can! Some Christians see prophecy as being super spiritual. However, I see it as something supernatural yet very attainable.

I commend you to move into the supernatural. For example, the other day, I was with some Christian girls visiting our church and the Lord impressed upon me to speak to one specifically after I prophesied over all of them. The Lord told me three times that the girl was truly beautiful. To me, she was an average sort of girl and she apparently assumed she was plain.

Jesus told me to tell her that He considers her beautiful and attractive. I shared that with her and it brought tears to her eyes. She wept as Jesus told her that she was not only beautiful inside in her heart, but she was beautiful to look at. She'd been lied to by the enemy for a long time saying that she was plain and saying that she wasn't beautiful and attractive. It's those fresh words from the Holy Spirit, fresh words from Jesus that really touch hearts.

You have the capacity to hear from God intuitively; you have the ability to touch people. I commend you for it!

eighteen

Practice Before You Practice

What exactly do I mean by this statement? I mean and highly recommend that before you begin to move out in the prophetic, you need to develop confidence in your gift and your ability to prophesy over people.

I suggest that the best way to gain some confidence is to start applying your gift face to face, with some of your Christian *acquaintances* who attend your church. These people, to my mind, are the best people to practice the Word of Knowledge on and to prophesy over. You see, "acquaintances" are the people in your church who you may wave to, or acknowledge in a polite way, but you have not yet related to them, in the same way as you relate to your personal friends.

Because of this somewhat distant relationship, it's easier to move in the prophetic with these people. This is simply because when you're sharing things about their character and life, you're not sharing things you already know about them.

I believe that it's harder to receive accurate Words of Knowledge with a person you know really well, because you know *so much information already.* Personally, I find it much harder to be confident that the information received has come from God. Notwithstanding, with faith and experience in your gift, you can very successfully prophesy over people you know really well.

However, I don't make it a firm rule to avoid prophesying over my close friends! The Spirit of God has a message for everyone and He wouldn't want me to exclude anyone. When I advise you to practice with acquaintances, I do so, because I know from personal experience that your confidence in your gift and ability to prophecy will increase faster that way.

Growing in confidence in the prophetic is the major concern for most beginners. I know even today, I am encouraged when people say to me, "That was a very accurate word; it was on-point and meant a lot to me."

I still like to receive feedback that my words are accurate, on-point, and encouraging. If I'm in the anointing and prophetic words come out of my mouth, I am confident to know that I'm speaking the truth. I know that I speak only what is right and it's coming from the Holy Spirit.

Some people in the prophetic aren't that confident. They need constant feedback from people to say that they were accurate and they spoke correctly into the person's life. But the more you grow in the prophetic, the more you will come to realize that when the Spirit of Jesus speaks through you, that He speaks the truth through convicting and empowering words to people. What I love best is to minister in the prophetic face to face, with people in churches.

I once went to a church and the Lord led me to a certain man. I said to him that he was going through a hard trial. I told him that the reason for his trial was that the Lord presently had him in a refiner's fire and he would come forth as gold! I went on to say that not many people could understand his trial, so they had offered all kinds of advice on how to escape from it, or how to cope with it. Because of this, he was swaying from one thing to another. The Lord wanted him to settle himself, just be himself and to just do what he felt was right in his spirit.

To my astonishment, the man filled with tears. He was obviously quite touched by my words. I was amazed that being a total stranger to him, I could walk up to him and give him such a touching, prophetic word. Yet, now years later, it's something I have grown accustomed to seeing. But each time, I am very humbled by the experience – God's amazing grace constantly surprises me.

As you grow in your new gift, you'll be able to look at a certain person and a prophetic word will come into your heart. You'll be able to walk up to them and share that word. I encourage you to ask the Lord for one particular prophetic message, or even a couple of them, every week to share with Christians that you know, so you can practice. When you practice face to face with people, you will see their reactions and this will be your instant feedback.

When you share a prophetic word face to face to some people, their immediate facial expression will tell you how the word touched them. For example: their eyes may tear up; or they become quietly emotional when a prophetic word is shared. As I implied earlier, no verbal feedback is necessary. *You know* that your word has meant a lot to them.

I feel that feedback of any sort is very important. Especially as you step out and begin to minister in the prophetic. Even today, after all my years of operating in the prophetic, I still love to be told that my message was on target. Feedback is the very best way to gain confidence that you have spoken God's word. God's truth and His personal revelation, not only ministers to the hearer's spirit, but your own spirit will be ministered to as well. Prophecy is, therefore, a win/win experience for all concerned. No wonder God wants every Christian to do it!

Satan will have you believe that you're just making up your own words. Satan will have you believe that you're speaking just from your own mind and you're not speaking the truth. He'll attack you in so many ways. He'll tell you that you're just guessing at what the message is and he'll try all sorts of tactics to derail you from your prophetic ministry.

I want you to be encouraged that it's only through face-to-face practice with other Christians that you'll start to develop your gift and gain confidence: you will know in your spirit that when you speak prophetically, God truly speaks through you.

I want to warn you: before salvation, you were no threat whatsoever to Satan's kingdom. After salvation, you have definitely become a target on the enemy's radar screen! Therefore, when you begin to operate in the prophetic, know that you will be in a constant spiritual combat zone!

Therefore, I want you to always know that God would not have allowed you to proceed to this point in your own strength. He is the one who has been preparing your heart and leading you every step of the way. God fully equips in *every way*, those He calls! God is bigger, stronger and smarter than the enemy.

Yes, the prophetic IS a battleground! Satan will not quit his attacks! He will keep on trying to discourage you from sharing this gift with people. I share this truth, not to frighten you, but to prepare you! Jesus Christ on the Cross defeated the enemy once for all time. Satan is, therefore, a toothless tiger! Can you imagine a gummy tiger trying to devour its prey? All Satan can do is to try to intimidate Christians: so that they will feel powerless! But God wants us to know that every believer has authority in Jesus' Name over the devil. Therefore, as Christians, we are to know always that Satan's rightful place - is under our feet! That's where the Cross of Jesus put him, once and for all!

Also, as believers, we have God's promise that "Greater is He (Jesus) who is in us, than he (Satan) who is in the world." In Christ, we are more than conquerors, because the same Holy Spirit that raised Jesus from the dead dwells in us. Operate on the fact that when Jesus begins a good work in us, He is the One who completes the task. His Spirit in us, equips us to do His Kingdom business, which of course includes prophecy.

Therefore, once you step out into the prophetic, don't quit. Just keep pressing into God and keep praising Him for every person He leads you to speak to. Determine in your heart and spirit to practice, practice, and practice some more! The only way through Satan's barrage of attacks is to practice so much that you become extremely confident that you're delivering accurate prophetic words. God will never let you down, as you step out in faith.

Before you go and minister to strangers, before you go and minister to people on the street, I wholeheartedly suggest that you begin to practice with Christian acquaintances in your church.

nineteen

Growing in Confidence

As I've covered before, the more you practice, the more you grow in confidence. To move to the stage where I'm at in my prophetic gifting takes a lot of practice. Feedback is a very useful thing to have and I'd encourage you to ask people that you prophesy over for feedback on whether it was accurate and how it spoke to them.

Maybe you don't realize it, but there are many prophetic sites online. There are prophecy groups on Facebook where you can gain experience by giving prophecies, and people will give you feedback. But some people on these groups don't give very detailed feedback. They might just say, "Thank you that touched me."

As a beginner, you will want specific and detailed feedback on your prophetic words, so you know that you hit particular points and know where in your prophecy that you touched someone's heart. For this reason, face-to-face prophesies are the best form of feedback.

Operating in the prophetic is like any other new endeavor: the more you do it, the more skilled you become. I remember when I started to learn to water ski, I used to fall off quite often, but the more I practiced, the easier it became to initially take off and to actually ski for a short time. Gradually, with practice, I could go longer and longer distances before falling off. In a way, the same is true of prophecy.

Most endeavors in life have a downside. The prophetic downside is Satan's constant attacks: he heaps condemnation on you that your prophecy was not from God, or it had absolutely no impact on the person you were speaking to. After twenty years of ministering in this way, I can assure you that Satan has not given up attacking me. That is why I stress to you that good feedback is the key to developing confidence. The more confident you are, the more accurate you become.

I find the best way to counter Satan is not only spending time with God and receiving feedback from Jesus and the Father, but also actually stepping out and ministering in the prophetic and getting first hand feedback! You will reach a stage where you know that your words are accurate to the hearer and you won't need to receive as much feedback. I have now come to the stage that when prophetic words come out of my mouth: I absolutely know that my message is spot-on.

For instance, the other day, I was sharing with a girl who visited our church on a short-term mission trip. I shared with her that Matthew 5:6 says, "Blessed are the pure in heart, for they shall see God." I told her that she was pure in heart as God sees her that way already. I assured her that she doesn't have to do anything special, because God already sees her pure heart and He loves her. I told her that her entire life is devoted to God and because of that, her heart was pure. She was really touched. She just listened as the Lord spoke to her through me. I really felt that the Lord had physically touched me, as I began to minister to her face to face. It was awesome!

She was transfixed. It was like she was in a trance. She was spellbound listening to the Lord speaking to her through me. It was a very effective witness to me that there was a strong anointing pouring forth from my lips. I don't often see people fall into something like a trance listening to me. It was very effective in giving me confidence when I spoke to others later in the day.

I was speaking to one guy and he said, "Where are you getting this information?"

I said, "I have a gift of prophecy and God is telling me what to say." And he replied, "Well, tell me something else about myself." I told him.

He then said, "Tell me about my friend here. Tell him things about his life." So, I looked at his friend and my words surprised the two of them. They were blown away and absolutely shocked that I had this gift and this ability to speak into people's lives. Therefore, you too, will grow in your confidence as you practice more.

Like many people, I'm not very good at drawing. I can only draw stick figures! I'm not skilled in drawing because I've never taken the time to practice and learn *how* to draw. The same will be true of you in prophecy if you only give one person a prophecy each month. Your confidence will not have a chance to grow!

There would be at least a couple of people whom the Lord would like you to speak to weekly, at church. It'll grow to where you start to share evangelically with strangers on the street. Your confidence will soon grow so that you will speak to ten or even twenty people a week.

On a two-mile walk, you might stop and speak to five people and share with them the message that God has for you. Always bear in mind, you don't have to lead a person to Jesus. Allow the Holy Spirit to use you to bless people and to plant His seeds in their mind.

You will need your confidence when you minister to people that are strangers because they might not give you very detailed feedback. Often they'll just say, "Thank you for sharing" and they won't say anything else. Just understand that you will have caught them by surprise and they will need time to ponder your words to them.

twenty

Practice Makes Perfect

I've already covered this subject quite extensively. Just as I mentioned multiple times, the best part of a prophecy is the Word of Knowledge. It is only practice that really defines your gift and makes your gift exceptional!

However, there is another benefit to practicing your gift. Practice allows you to maintain God's peace, even when a difficult or strange situation comes your way. Only practice will allow you to handle these unusual and unexpected situations.

There are a minority of people in every city who are somewhat strange! I want you to know that God will cause you to meet some of these people and will lead you to minister to them. When this happens, it's only your past practice that will cause you to stay on target and have the wisdom to glorify God in that situation. Without practice, you will not have the confidence or ability to carry out God's will.

Practicing prophecy is essentially enabling you to exhibit God's love to all people by using the prophetic word with both those you know and complete strangers.

I can't stress it enough that Satan detests the prophetic. Instead of allowing him to pull you down, see his attacks as "you being a threat to his kingdom." The best way to combat his accusation that you are speaking from your own mind is to practice your gift, so that you will receive confirmation through feedback on the prophetic words that you've *already* done.

I've been ministering in the prophetic for about seventeen to twenty years. During that time, I estimate that I would have delivered at least ten thousand prophetic words to people and about three-quarters of them would have been strangers. Yet, I can tell you that my confidence still takes some battering when I deliver a very extensive prophetic word to a person and they don't give any type of feedback.

Sometimes, the word has been so extensive that I really needed some kind of feedback from the person, because God says that He is going to do so many awesome things in their Christian life. I know there is no point being disappointed because every person is unique. They would have had no idea that I was going to approach them like I did and often, they may be in shock at what I have said to them.

Yet, after all this time, I do sometimes get discouraged! At times, I still doubt my ability in the prophetic and think that I didn't deliver God's message right. This is my reason that I underline the importance of practice and also why I want you to be aware of Satan's attacks.

I believe that you can reach a stage of maturity in the prophetic office, when God may increase your anointing, so that you actually become a prophet.

I realize that not every believer will agree with my theology when I say that, and that's okay. I am aware of the fivefold office of ministry, namely: Apostle, Prophet, Evangelist, Pastor and Teacher, but I personally believe that we need to gradually grow into these definite ministries.

I also believe that there's a higher accuracy, and a higher level of anointing placed on your words, even if you weren't called to be a prophet. Therefore, practice can allow you to reach an ability level in your gift that allows you to call things out and summarize a person's entire life: there comes a level of maturity in the prophetic, where you can give prophetic words that are very extensive and which sum up all the prior prophecies that the person has received.

A prophetic person should be anointed. They should be in the anointing, to deliver a prophetic word! Sometimes, I don't feel particularly anointed and I still may deliver a prophetic word to someone when God prompts me to do so. What I am saying is to trust God's prompting and don't be put off by your actual feelings at the time. Sometimes, I come from home and I haven't done anything special other than talking to the Lord on the way to the train and yet, the Lord will graciously give me someone to minister to on the train!

It's important to be anointed, but that's something that only God can do. Your part is to ask God to prepare you and to guide you to the people of His choice and then, to practice your gift. One way to practice your gift – as I impart the gift later in the book – is to prophesy over me.

The difference between prophesying over someone else and prophesying over me is: I'll take your prophecy apart, line by line in order to give you honest feedback. I will tell you how it touched me. I promise that I will really encourage you!

I feel it would almost be a waste of time reading through this whole book, and not do the practical application, by not prophesying over me! I ask this, not because I lack personal prophecies, but I sincerely want to encourage you! I just know how encouraging I can be and how I can move people into the prophetic.

I can also have you prophesy over friends and people I know and receive feedback from them too. Practice makes perfect!

twenty-one

Ready to Go

Some of what I have shared so far in this book are:

- Prophetic Evangelism is something you have to decide to do.
- The Lord will give you the gift of prophecy and the ability to receive prophetic words for strangers.
- The Lord is the source of prophetic words. You can't go around giving accurate prophetic words to strangers if the Lord isn't providing the words.

However, the fact that you are reading this book tells me that there will be a time when you will be ready to step out into Prophetic Evangelism. Therefore, why not contemplate stepping out now, while you are being encouraged with what I am sharing? Tell the Lord that you want Him to use you to give His words to others.

It's important to understand that knowledge is only good if it's practiced. There's much wisdom in the Bible, but wisdom is only effective when you practice it. Many people can quote scriptures, but it is only those who live by those quotes who will actually benefit from them.

Although I still have many things to share with you in this book, you have enough information to go out and to practice prophecy. I also want you to remember two important things: you are deeply loved and God has led you to read this book. These two facts should tell you that God is encouraging you and He is wanting you to step out and to begin to prophetically evangelize people by sowing "seeds" into their life that will ultimately bring glory to God.

I'll share a quick example with you.

When I was about to board a train last Sunday, I stepped back to let a girl step on before me. Then I went down and sat in front of her. The Lord told me He had a message for her and that He wanted me to prophesy over her. He said to me, "Before you can become a champion in life and really achieve in your life, you've got to first believe that you are a champion yourself."

I turned around and shared that with her, and had about a ten-minute conversation with her. Towards the end of our conversation, she shared with me that before I turned around, she was just thinking about a particular career and whether she was going to be a success.

The word that God had given me to say to her was really timely! She'd only just been thinking about the subject of success when I turned around. God's always ready for you to step out! There are people passing you daily, whom God can give a prophetic word to.

I look forward to the day when hundreds of people are downloading and reading this book. I'm looking forward to receiving testimonies from all over the world of people who were ready to go, who were ready to step out in Prophetic Evangelism, and who were ready to seriously make an impact on the world that they live in.

Many people are just sad, lonely and depressed! They live lives of quiet desperation and they're not excited at all about their own life. They're lacking vision and purpose. Many unbelievers don't know the reason for their existence. Those of us who move in Prophetic Evangelism are sent as messengers to go and shine a light on the reason that people are living and give them encouragement.

I look forward to an army of people rising up in every suburb and in every city around the world, perhaps thousands of people each day, all receiving messages from God! It's for that reason that I have put my time, my effort and my resources into making this book.

twenty-two

Preparing to Witness

It's wonderful to be in the anointing, or to feel the presence of God over your life before you go out to share with people prophetically. But if you're someone who can wake-up, have a shower, and you already feel the presence of God, that's fine. That's a great way to be prepared, because you really need to be in the presence to minister.

Last year, instead of just encountering people and prophesying over them as I went about life, I especially organized to meet up with other like-minded friend, to go for an hour, witnessing with him to whomever God led us to. On that occasion, I purposely spent some time with God and also some time in worship. If you're going out to make an active effort, then it's advisable to get yourself in the anointing. This entails having a presence of mind that allows you to just know that He is with you. To me personally, feeling the presence of God is very similar to when I am worshipping at church each week.

Nevertheless, I confess that quite often, I haven't felt particularly anointed by God. Yet, the Lord still pointed a person out to me and He still graced my life to allow me to walk up to them and give them a prophetic word!

Every believer is to know that their "feelings" don't always give an accurate report about a situation. This is because our feelings are part of our soul area. Our soul and our actual physical body comprise our fleshly or carnal nature. Therefore fleshly "feelings" cannot be fully trusted! This is because Satan can easily manipulate them! However, Satan cannot ever, ever, touch your born-again spirit! This fact is so comforting to know!

If you're going to make a concerted effort to evangelize, specifically for a long period of the day or night, you do need to take the time to prepare. Sometimes, you can also achieve great results, simply by Jesus gracing you with His presence and a message, then, carrying that message through with His anointing on the word. A friend illustrated this point once to me. He said:

"There's definitely something about you Matthew. I could approach the same person and say the same things that you say, but I would have a different result than the reaction that you receive. There's definitely something happening with you and there's definitely a spiritual connection with what you're doing."

That's the grace I'm talking about, when I said that Jesus will grace you with His anointing for the message. When you receive a message from the Lord, it comes with a particular grace. It is His grace that allows a message to be heard, and to cause His anointing to fall onto the person. This anointing prepares the person to be open to the message and to receive it with gladness and thankfulness.

Many people who hear a word from me, thank me for the message and they also thank me for taking the time to share it with them. Some people are more thankful than others. Some people are really glad and genuinely take time to express their thanks and joy that I shared the message with them. Some are less so. This type of fluctuation tells me that just as everyone's character differs, so too, is their level of understanding and their walk with God. We are all on different levels of spirituality and that's fine, because everyone on this planet is individually and very uniquely wired by God. He has a definite purpose and a plan for every life.

So many people that I share a prophetic message with are not yet walking with God. Perhaps God has not entered their mind for a very long time. So when someone delivers a somewhat spiritual message to them, sometimes it's not received with as much joy as a Christian would receive the same message. However, they are still very polite and thankful and they do express their thanks for sharing the message.

It's the same thing with how people would express their thanks over a meal. Some would express more thanks than others. It's simply up to where the person is standing with God.

If you're going out with a friend and you're planning to prophetically evangelize, I'd suggest that you put on some worship music and sing to the Lord for some time. By doing so, you will feel the presence of the Lord come upon you and you will be ready to walk in His anointing. Then go out and share your message with the people God has already prepared for you.

twenty-three

Ready All the Time

As I discussed already, most times, when I give a prophetic message to a stranger, it's while I'm doing my ordinary business. For instance, I serve homeless people who visit our Salvation Army community center. I serve free coffee, tea, and hot chocolate to the public mostly on Wednesday to Friday afternoons. Therefore, I deal with quite a few people and from time-to-time, I give one of my customers a prophetic message. Also, on my travel to and from work, I meet different strangers and God often prompts me to give a prophetic message to someone.

Sometimes, as I'm walking down a street, towards the train station to and from my place of work, I meet people and God may point one of them out to me to give a prophetic message to. In fact, I can never be sure when God is going to reveal a person to me. That's because I am always available!

Be assured that there are always people wherever you go, or whatever you're doing that God wants to speak to. It's good to develop an attitude within yourself to be always available, to minister to people according to the leading of the Lord.

Most people would be totally unaware, but I've been in a depression for ten weeks. During that time of depression, I was still available to the Lord, to share messages with strangers and was still just as effective as when I am not in depression. It proves to me that really, it's all about God's enabling power! Therefore, it doesn't matter whether you feel up to it or not, God never changes and His grace is always sufficient for you.

It's a wonderful thing when you can be used by God anytime and anyplace to share a message with a stranger. You may only have one opportunity to deliver that message to that person. Or, it's possible that you could miss God's call one day and not share the message, but the next day, God organizes the same person to again meet up with you and you could share it then.

It's important that you know that there's always various degrees of fear and trepidation when sharing a prophetic word and we'll talk about that in later chapters. But if you miss a prophetic word, or if you're too scared to deliver it, then sometimes as I have already said, the Lord can arrange for you to meet that person again. Alternately, the Lord may decide to minister to that person in another way. The point is: *you are never to feel guilty about it!* God never inflicts guilt, it is Satan who is manipulating your soul, so reject his onslaught!

The more you experience moving in the prophetic, the more experienced you'll become. Therefore, it's a good thing to be ready all the time. Maybe you could make a point of asking the Holy Spirit to keep you in the state of being able to smile and welcome people, regardless of how you are particularly "feeling!" Also, be courteous and be well mannered by saying a simple 'thanks' and 'please' wherever appropriate.

Understand that God is always in control! When you grow in experience and when you grow in love, you'll find that you'll be always available - to give a prophetic word!

twenty-four

Picking the Stranger

With Prophetic Evangelism, you need to understand how the Lord identifies a person to whom He wants you to give a message to. I heard the best explanation from another person and it seemed to sit very well with me. I have shown this method to a couple of others and it worked for them as well.

Imagine that you're in a submarine and you put up a periscope above the water. You turn the periscope around and as you scan the surrounding sea, you spot a boat. The periscope doesn't just stay focused on the boat. It keeps going around and then it comes back to again focus on that boat. The same is true when you're looking across a crowd of people, and one person seems to be standing out. To you, their face seems to be shining more than that of the other people. If you do another sweep of the room, and come back to that person, and that person is still standing out somehow, then that's a good sign that the Lord is picking out a stranger for you, to give a prophetic word to.

I have to warn you that sometimes, you may find the other person physically attractive. This is normal, but Satan may lie to you and say, "You're only looking at that person because you find them attractive!"

I've discovered that the best way to test if this attractive person is really highlighted by the Holy Spirit: is to ask the Holy Spirit for a prophetic word for them. If the Holy Spirit gives you a word for them, then you can be sure, even though they are attractive or handsome to you, that the Lord indeed wants you to minister to them. You will then become more confident that the Lord has actually picked them out for you, to give them His message.

The Lord has shared with me on many occasions that even attractive people need to be ministered to. In fact, God shared with me that sometimes physically attractive people really need encouragement about what kind of person they are on the inside, because they receive so many compliments about their physical appearance!

On the whole then, when you've identified a person, a simple way to test whether you've identified the right person is to ask the Lord for the beginnings of the prophetic word that you're to share with the stranger. Then you can approach them! One thing that will happen, when you've identified a stranger and you have a prophetic word for them, is that fear of approaching them might come up inside you. That is the subject of our next chapter.

twenty-five

Conquering Fear

When you're in the business of doing Prophetic Evangelism and approaching strangers on the streets, there will often come a fear of man – a fear that will well up within you when you identify a stranger and as you contemplate approaching them.

That awful fear is there! You feel heavy everywhere! I want you to be aware that fear can come from natural sources, but in times like this, it usually comes from Satan himself! This fear is designed to stop you from delivering the prophetic word. The fear has all sorts of connotations to it like, "Who are you to go and approach that stranger? That word you have may not be true! You will just make a fool of yourself! You are having yourself on - you are just making it all up!"

There are all kinds of things that come into your mind, but the only way to test whether the word is true, is to approach the stranger and tell them what God has told you. You'll find usually that your word was spot on and the fear was just something that was trying to discourage you from your assignment. Remember, it says in scripture that "perfect love casts out all fear."

One very simple way to conquer fear is to ask the Lord for the message that He has for the person, then, picture yourself being the receiver. Think to yourself, what if a total stranger came and shared that message with me? Would I feel encouraged? You'll find usually that the prophetic word you've been given is very encouraging and you would be interested in hearing it. Well, I want you to know that the same is true for that stranger, whom you haven't yet approached.

Often, I'll invite the Lord to speak the prophetic word directly to me. I will then ponder that word and let the love of Christ well up within me for the stranger. For example: "How are they going to feel when they hear this? Will it be good news to them?"

Now, the fear of man is something you simply have to overcome. This is because it normally comes from Satan and he is never going to really back away! I found after years of sharing messages to strangers, that only recently, the fear seems to have somewhat diminished in my life.

I think the reason the fear has reduced is because I'm starting to mentor people and take them on the road with me, teaching them the art of Prophetic Evangelism. Therefore, I think that the Lord just removed Satan's attacks on my life, so I can have more of a covering.

Be encouraged that fear is a very natural thing even though it sometimes comes from a supernatural power. For example: If you were going to walk up to a stranger, and ask them out on a date, you would still experience fear! The same fear would come if you approached a stranger to find out their name and address. There's just a natural fear we have in approaching strangers and saying certain things to them.

Satan doesn't like the prophetic word: he doesn't like people being touched by God. He'll use any method he can, and any thought he can in order to distract you from your mission of delivering a message which will bring clarity or comfort to a total stranger.

Always be aware that he or one of his demons will be there! Be aware that he'll bring some kind of fear in you. Learn the method of receiving a prophetic word from Jesus and pondering it, and thinking how it will bless the person to whom you're going to give it. I find that often, the word I am to deliver gives me much comfort and this conquers the fear as I ponder it.

I shared a couple of chapters ago that I was on a train and an attractive girl sat behind me. I had a fear of turning around and talking to her. I didn't want to seem as if I was someone trying to flirt with her. But it was the Lord, who wanted me to give her a message about her being a success. It was that prophetic word that swelled in my heart and gave me the love for her that made me turn around, and thereby conquer the fear that had welled up in my heart. Be encouraged that the fear *will* present itself and then conquer the fear, the way I've told you to.

twenty-six

The Prophetic Word

Let's imagine that you have the gift of prophecy - and you have been prophesying over people you know, but now you are contemplating reaching out to strangers, how will you go about it?

I suggest that you tell God that you are ready for the next step! Ask Him to point out particular strangers to you, whom He has a message for. You will then need to just wait to receive His prompting in your spirit. When He does prompt you, straight away, briefly scan over the people surrounding you, once or twice. You will in the process, find yourself to be drawn to one person.

I personally find that this one particular person will have a faint glow around them. After you spot them, silently ask the Lord, "Is that the one?" He will confirm in your heart that it is! At this stage, He will probably tell you part of the prophetic word He has for them.

Now it's "crunch-time" – you need to approach the stranger! Realize, however, that just knowing some of God's message for them will conquer most of your fears. In fact, at this stage, your heart will begin to actually warm towards this person. I know that my particular approach line was given to me by the Holy Spirit, so if He doesn't give you a personal introduction line, perhaps you can use my method.

I walk straight up to them, even if they are talking to a friend. I get their attention by saying, "Excuse me." And when they look at me, I say, "Excuse me. I have a special gift, and from time to time, that gift allows me to get a message for a person. Today, just now, I've received a message for you." If there are two people listening, I look directly at my target and say, "Would you like to hear it?" They mostly agree!

Often, the first thing I do is to launch into the prophetic word with a Word of Knowledge. For example, *it could be something like this*: "You're a person who has a tremendous ability to care for others – your emotions run really deep. If you see a TV documentary on Africa, showing starving children with swollen bellies, it's something so sensitive and emotional to you that you turn the television off. You simply can't handle watching disturbing things when you cannot physically change the circumstances."

I would perhaps continue with another Word of Knowledge. "You also have a very generous heart. You don't hold back from helping people. You're a very confident person who is also very sensitive to the needs of others. From time to time, when people approach you on the street, you'll discreetly give some money to them. You don't make a big deal about it, but you're a person who is very confident and very willing to give to people less fortunate than yourself."

After you've launched into Words of Knowledge, the person will inwardly know that something supernatural is happening. They will be waiting to find out what you are going to say next.

After you've spoken these Words of Knowledge, the prophetic tap starts – I like to call it a tap. You switch on this tap just by speaking out what comes into your mind about them. Just let the tap flow! Continue to speak according to what the Holy Spirit gives you. You will see in their eyes or by their mannerism that they're paying attention to you.

However, at this point, if you see them getting a little uncomfortable, just stop speaking! Quietly bless them and thank them for listening.

Words of Knowledge usually grab a person's full attention. Take your time because God may also have Words of Wisdom to pass on to the person. He may have special directions for them to follow, in order for the prophecy to come true in their lives. It's also around this time that you can deliver the prophecy part of the word, by speaking about their current life, or by speaking about their life in the future.

If you begin to tell them what they should do, (by giving them Words of Wisdom) or even if you tell them something about their future, *without first giving them the Words of Knowledge,* then God's directions for them won't hold as much weight or authority.

This is because the person has no personal evidence to prove that you're actually bringing a true message from God to them. All they have really is what *you're* saying to them! Regardless of how polite they may seem at the time, once they walk away, they will put the whole matter behind them and ignore your words. That's why the Word of Knowledge is so vital.

If you receive a good response, tell them that God loves them and that's the reason why He has given you a prophetic word for them. They may ask if they can contact you again, and by all means, give them your contact number. (I carry a few simple business cards in my wallet for this purpose.)

If you receive a negative response from people, just say: "That's okay! I'm sorry if I have upset you, I won't hold you up any longer. God Bless." However, if they are still negative to you, don't let it upset you. Just know that some people have evil spirits, and that's just an evil spirit reacting to the anointing that's in your life! Just brush it off and don't worry about it anymore. That's par for the course. That's one of the consequences of entering into a spiritual war.

Sometimes, there will be negative experiences! But I reckon I only have a negative experience, or get a negative response from one in a hundred people. Therefore, if you get a few of them in a row, just know that it's just Satan trying to shut you down. Don't worry about that!

My friend and I were out doing Prophetic Evangelism last week, and we had three people we approached who didn't want to hear what we wanted to say.

The first one we had a word for, the guy talked on the phone, then he disappeared into a bar. We went in to go to the bar, so he came out again and we gave the prophetic word to him. We could have easily given up on that one. But if God gives you a prophetic word, often, He really wants you to deliver that word, so it's good to persist. God will lead you to do the right thing!

The next person we tried to approach didn't want to talk to us and the third person we approached said he couldn't speak English, so we just said we'd pray for him. It's possible to receive a prophetic word when the person really doesn't want to hear it. You just brush that off and keep going.

I often close a message by saying that I'm a prophet and I have the gift of prophecy and God wanted them to know that message. Sometimes, I'll ask them what their first name is, so I can pray for them. Sometimes, I ask them is there anything else they'd like to know, but if you just close it in a polite and casual way, it lets them know that they're loved.

Like me, if you have business cards made up with your name and phone number on them and just the words, "Prophetic Evangelist" on the front, you can close your encounters with certain people by giving them a card and inviting them to contact you at any time with their questions. I'd say that I hand out one card to twenty or so people I talk to. Your card could also have a website with information on how to become a Christian or what Christianity is all about.

twenty-seven

Handling Post Word Attacks

You already know by now that Satan hates the prophetic! Therefore, you will meet spiritual opposition when you go out and encourage Christians in their everyday walk with a prophetic word. Our enemy, the devil, is even more upset when you give a non-Christian a prophetic word that may lead them closer to Christ.

It's been my personal belief, and it was reinforced to me through a prophetic word, that when I give prophetic words to strangers, that those words, however brief, will assist them in some way in their progress towards full salvation. I say this, because I firmly believe that the Holy Spirit knows those who will become Christians in the future, and He is actually highlighting people for me to give a stepping-stone into their ultimate salvation experience. In fact, my earnest belief in this theory, continually stirs me up to keep on track and not to ever give up.

Because of Satan's strong dislike of the prophetic, he goes out of his way to attack those who operate in it. He will tell you that your prophetic words were not true, or that you are a total loser! He may tell you that the only reason why you approach people with such ridiculous words is because you are lonely. So be prepared for any of his detrimental attacks on you and in the name and the authority of Jesus Christ, command him to be quiet!

The best ongoing way to overcome Satan is to have confidence in your gift and to know that when God gives you a prophetic word, that it's a true word from Him. Know that you have a truly wonderful gift and you are genuinely encouraging people to know that God loves them.

Satan doesn't announce himself: he's not quite that stupid! He doesn't announce himself and say, "Hi. This is Satan speaking." No, he just drops his crushing thoughts into your head. He will tell you that what you said to the stranger was not coming from God, but just your own mind. He will actually accuse you of purposely building up a person's hope for nothing! He will tell you to stop deceiving innocent people with all your rubbish about having a prophetic gift!

When in the past, I have started to think that I was a desperately lonely person with no genuine friends or that I should stop interrupting people's lives by giving false words to them, then I knew beyond doubt that the devil had been having his way with me. Now, I recognize his style much easier, when he first starts to say something nasty about me.

Be warned: If you allow his evil attacks to have a place in your life, you will stop giving prophetic words. My suggestion for you is to just keep pressing on, regardless!

twenty-eight

Prophesying with friends

It's a good thing to let your friends know that you have a prophetic gift and that sometimes you give a prophetic word to strangers. It's also a good thing to encourage your friends to sometimes stand with you when you give prophetic words to people.

I have a particular friend who becomes embarrassed if I give a prophetic word to a stranger. Whenever I stop to talk to someone, he will continue to walk ahead and will stand some distance away, until I've finished giving the word. I would much prefer it if he stood with me and could listen to the prophetic word and perhaps add something that he feels God wants him to add.

Therefore, if you have friends with you, just let them know in advance that you will be doing Prophetic Evangelism if the opportunity presents itself. Explain to them that they have liberty at any time to add to the prophetic word if they feel led to. I say this because sometimes, the Holy Spirit can speak some very meaningful things to a friend, and they can share something that actually means more to the person than the prophetic word that you may give.

For example: Last week before church, a new friend accompanied me and my regular prophetic mate to do some Prophetic Evangelism. I extended to her the same liberty, that when she hears us give God's message to a stranger, to go ahead and share whatever's on her heart. I told her that when we finish a prophetic word, we would ask her if she had anything to add. She was only a new friend and I didn't want her to feel obligated in any way to give a word herself. But if she had a word, I'll give her the opportunity to share it.

We have since gone out again as a threesome, and out of five different encounters, she had something to add three times! In fact, she was really comfortable about it. After one prophetic word we gave to a woman, my mate and I went to the restrooms, and when we came back, my new friend stopped and went to the woman that we had earlier spoken to. She shared something with that woman for a couple of minutes. When she came back to us, we were really happy that not only was she hearing prophetic words herself from God, but she was also confident to add to our initial word! It was thrilling for all of us to know that God had further things to say to that particular woman.

If you find that a friend is uncomfortable, then ask them to stand aside and wait. But if this friend really has no patience at all for Prophetic Evangelism, just politely tell them it would be better for all concerned if they don't come out with you.

Personally, I am extremely committed to what I do. Therefore, I make it plain to those who are with me that they can choose to take part or to stand aside. When you regularly receive God's prophetic words to pass on to people, it's a good thing not to be holding them back just because you have friends that are uncomfortable.

That's how I deal with all my friends, and I pray that you've gleaned some knowledge from this.

twenty-nine

Making a lifestyle of it

What do I mean to make a lifestyle of it? I mean that whenever you leave your house, after spending time with God, you're ready to give prophetic words to strangers. You need to be open all the time, wherever you are! Whenever you are waiting in a line to be served, be aware of others in the line. It could be in a post office, at the ATM machine, a coffee shop, a movie theater queue, or wherever there is a line. Be ready at any time for God to prompt you.

When you're in a shop buying a drink from a convenience store, be aware that the person behind the counter needs encouragement. Tell them to have a good day or ask them questions about how their day is going and just be an encouragement.

As I go about my daily routine, I find that I am always encouraging and having dialogue with people. Wherever I am, I'm starting conversations with people, and sometimes, I can move into the prophetic. I find that even in the middle of a conversation I can share prophetic things with people. Just be aware that if you make a lifestyle of always being open and always being ready to give prophetic words, you and others are always blessed.

David, my long time prophetic friend, and I, decided to do an hour of prophetic street ministry each week before church. I found that a time-frame- restriction was hard for me to initially adjust to. It felt very strange but after only a few weeks, I was quite comfortable about it.

When you have told God that you are available at any time to do prophetic ministry, it's important to be happy and be on top of your game! At times, you may be feeling quite depressed or sick in some other way, so that's quite understandable to want some time out.

However, if you're not depressed or sick, but you are simply not in the mood to do ministry, it's best to be upfront with God. He knows about it already, but it's a good time to ask Him to help you change your mood. When He sees your heart, He will find a way to cheer you up. I find it best to purposely ask the Lord each morning for His fresh grace and anointing for me to have opportunities to share my faith and prophesy.

When you habitually give prophetic words to strangers over a long time, it becomes part of your character. It actually becomes a lifestyle! Therefore, when it's a lifestyle, it's so much easier to carry on doing it. By having a prophetic lifestyle, it's both easier to share with others, and to encourage beginners to do likewise.

Even before I had my planned sessions with David, I was giving ten to twenty prophetic words a week. It's just part of my life; it's what I do! I am constantly sowing seeds into people's lives to encourage them to come closer to God. I wish I could inspire thousands of people to give prophetic words to strangers. My desire is that this book will inspire many Christians to give prophecy a go!

thirty

Finding Your Motivation

Personal motivation to share the good news of Jesus Christ through Prophetic Evangelism must always come from the Holy Spirit within us. It must never come from a sense of "religious obligation" on our part. We should always be conscious that God loves us first and foremost for - *who we already are in Christ, and not for the things that we do for Him.*

Many people with the gift of prophecy use their gift to build themselves up, rather than to build others up. They go around encouraging people with the gift of prophecy to make themselves feel good! (I know this because I have often done it myself.)

The correct motivation to do Prophetic Evangelism is twofold: to build Jesus' Kingdom on earth, and to encourage people to draw closer to Him.

Some people, who go to outreaches to learn how to witness on the street, may have the motivation of doing God a favor. But I want you to know that this kind of attitude comes from "religion" and not the Holy Spirit! People with this kind of attitude, not only bring a Gospel of gloom to the people they preach to, but they often judge other Christians who don't do likewise.

Whilst many zealous and well-meaning street "evangelists" have good intentions for doing what they do, some have an unhealthy mind disposition that Satan has planted. Therefore, like any form of street evangelism, we need people to enter the ministry of Prophetic Evangelism in the right state of mind and not out of guilt, pride or a negative spirit.

Love must be the prime motivation to move in this gift. Love conquers the hearts of all. Love puts the devil to flight! Satan loves to heap negativity onto everyone, but people need to know that God in very interested in their private life, because He loves them and wants the best for them and their whole family.

Therefore, God wants us to be comfortable and at peace in our identity in Christ. He wants us to hear His voice and be led by Him. God doesn't love you more when you're doing Prophetic Evangelism. Actually, God loves us, whoever we are, no matter what we're doing! If you're not confident that God loves you just for being you, then you need to seek teaching on that truth. You need to understand that you're highly favored and highly loved by God. It's from this personal knowledge of God's extravagant love for us that empowers us to love and to minister to others.

We can be filled with the Holy Spirit's presence to such a state that we have an overflow of His love for others. It's out of this overflow that we're meant to minister: it's out of this constant love within us that we're meant to minister to others.

It's good to know that God loves us! It's also good to know that He enjoys us doing things that we were created to do. We learn from the book of Ephesians that we were created to do good works. These good works were planned by God long before we were even conceived! Moving in Prophetic Evangelism is one of many good works that God would *delight* in you doing.

The very fact that you're reading this book up to this point means that you are open for God to use in this way. The only requirement is to have an intimate relationship with the Lord Jesus so that you can hear His voice, and that you have a genuine desire to help others to know His awesome love as well.

If you start to minister out of any sense of lacking in yourself, or by trying to impress God through a sense of religion, recognize that they are wrong motivations. Sure, the Lord will still use you. Sure, the Lord will give you prophetic words to give to people, but it's not a healthy relationship for you to be in with the Lord.

It's good to know that when you're sharing things prophetically with strangers from day to day and week to week, that you're a weapon – you're a real weapon in God's artillery – used strategically to take down the enemy's ground and to make progress for God in the lives of total strangers. You are an enemy of Satan, because you really are a weapon that's being used.

You will face attack, and I've talked about attacks before. You *will* face attacks from Satan. He'll try to have a go at your confidence and tell you that you're not really good, or that you are doing it for the wrong reasons.

Please don't take this chapter as a sense of saying you're doing it for the wrong reasons. I want you to know that God loves you and He wants to use you and you're going to be a real spiritual weapon against Satan and his demons. Take all that positivity aboard, so that you know deep in your spirit that your motivation is great and you will be very effective in Prophetic Evangelism!

thirty-one

Prophesying to a group of people

You may approach a group of people and only have a prophecy for one of them. After you finish prophesying to the particular individual, another person in the group may ask you for a prophecy as well. When this second person asks for a prophecy, the Lord will grace you with a word for them also. This may continue in this way, all the way around the group of people and you could spend up to twenty minutes with them.

Sometimes, I'm inspired to approach a group of people and tell them that I have a gift and I can tell something about each of the people in the group. On those occasions, I deliver a prophetic word – a Word of Knowledge – to each of the people in the group.

For one, I might say, "You're a really giving person. You're a person who is quite able to give of your money without hassles. Many times you've given money to people that others wouldn't. God is very happy with you. Therefore, He allows you to have enough money for you to share with others." Then to another I might say, "You are a scholar. The Lord has given you special ability to work with and understand things that many others can't."

You can just go around the group giving each a prophetic Word of Knowledge. You can go on and say what people are called to do with their life, and it just opens an opportunity to minister to several people. The Holy Spirit will lead you.

Someone in the group may say that your Word of Knowledge wasn't quite right. This is the time that you make sure they understood you correctly. Have the person who challenged you explain to you, what they think they heard. Most times they have misunderstood what you said. If this is so, then rephrase the Word of Knowledge in a simpler way. From the people who have challenged me about this, most of them, I have discovered, had originally misunderstood what I first said to them. The more that you do prophetic words in groups, the more fun it is.

Always let people know that God is the source of your prophetic words and that you're not a clairvoyant, medium, or psychic. It's good for them to understand that God delivered the word to them so they can give God the praise and the glory in the future.

Wherever you go, if God's leading you to give a prophetic word, just be confident that you're right. Don't be walking around wondering whether you're right! Your confidence in the prophetic word is shown on your face and in the tone of your voice. If you're hesitant or scared in giving a word, you'll find your lack of confidence brushes off on people. This causes them to be less receptive to what you're saying to them. However, if you confidently and boldly approach people, most of them will listen to what you have to say. Even if you're a little nervous inside, that's okay; it's your outer confidence that carries the prophetic word.

Prophesying to groups is a good and fun thing. It's entertaining for everybody in the group. God really uses me in that area many times. Sometimes, when I'm finished prophesying to a group, I'll ask any of them if they have a question for Jesus. Often, someone will come forth with a question. Normally, the first question they ask is a fairly simple one, just testing to know that you really hear from Jesus. Then the second question they ask is more serious like, "How's my mother going?" Or, perhaps they'll ask more pointed questions such as: "My mother died last year. Is she in a good place?"

In all these times, Jesus could tell me what their relative was up to. Feel free to open it up for questions. If you're confident, that you can hear from Jesus, He will surely answer everyone's questions.

thirty-two

Time for action

You can read a book like this and be encouraged by what is said. You can learn that the gift of prophecy is available for every born-again person. You can learn all about prophesying to strangers, but all of that information is pointless if you don't take action personally.

Yes, the reason for this book is for people to be educated about giving prophetic words to strangers, but this book is only useful to you if you take advantage of that knowledge and go ahead and prophesy to strangers.

In the next chapter, I'm going to pray a prayer for you to receive the gift of prophecy. Then, I'm going to encourage you to write to me at my e-mail address, or on Facebook – just send me a message and prophesy over me. I encourage all of you to do that. Believe me, I'm the best judge of your prophetic word. Don't be scared of prophesying over someone who's an established prophet. I want to be here for you to prophesy over, and I want you to draw from the Holy Spirit, the courage to prophesy over me so I can give you extensive feedback. I'll show you what gifts: Words of Knowledge, Words of Wisdom, or Words of Prophecy, are in operation in the actual prophecy you give me.

It's time to act guys. It's not the time to rest on your laurels. It's not the time to put this book away and say, "Gee! That was a good book. I'll look at it another time when I'm going to start to prophesy." No, it's time now, while this knowledge is fresh and new to you, to rise up and defeat procrastination. Today, right now, take the opportunity to pray the impartation prayer and then trust the Holy Spirit to lead you as you prophesy over me.

thirty-three

Impartation prayer for prophecy

If you follow my directions in this chapter with action, you will receive the gift of Prophesy and God's anointing, so that you will be able to prophesy over me.

First, we'll start with the prayer. If you want to read this prayer and then pray it, then the gift of prophecy will come upon you. I've had about three hundred people pray this prayer, and about ninety-nine percent of them prophesied over me correctly. The remaining one percent, probably received the gift, but they didn't have the courage to prophesy over me. I encourage you to first carefully read this prayer. Then I want you to pray this prayer, and then prophesy over me.

Dear Father, I come before you humbly as an eager servant. I agree that You have three gifts of prophecy – word of wisdom, word of knowledge, and prophecy – and I ask you today for those three gifts to manifest in my life. I know that the Apostle Paul said we should pursue the spiritual gifts and especially the gift of prophecy. He actually said that we should covet the gift of prophecy, that we should earnestly desire it. He said that prophecy was the best gift! Bearing all that in mind, I ask for the three gifts of prophecy be given to me in my life today and be witnessed through me as I prophesy over Matthew or someone else to receive feedback. In Jesus' name I ask. Amen.

Now, if you have earnestly prayed that prayer, I really encourage you to prophesy over me. I find that my best way to move into the anointing is to put on some worship music and get the lyrics of the songs and sing the songs for half an hour until you feel the presence of

God come upon you. This will be similar to when you feel the presence of God during corporate worship time at church.

Alternatively, open up your Bible and read it until you feel the presence of God come to you or enter into prayer for twenty to thirty minutes until you feel the presence of God come to you. You can incorporate one method I have suggested or any combination of those three methods.

Therefore, go to a quiet place and prepare yourself now. Don't just put down the book and say, "That was great." When you've finished the last chapter of the book, possibly come back to this and prepare yourself and receive the anointing in your life. Once you feel the presence of God in your life, open your email and send an email to me or send me a personal message on Facebook with the prophecy.

Now, simply allow the presence of God to rest on you, then open an email and say, "Dear Matthew, I feel the Lord wants to say this to you." When you've typed that sentence, another sentence will appear in your mind. Just type out what appears in your mind, and when you've finished that sentence another sentence will appear in your mind, so type out that sentence. Now, as you're typing, when you're two or three sentences in, you'll get the thought that you're just making this up, and this is just coming from you, and it's not really a prophecy at all, so you'll become nervous. Don't worry about any of those thoughts. Those things originated from Satan and he is pushing them into your mind. So ignore his onslaught.

Continue typing. Get a couple of paragraphs of prophecy, then, God will stop giving you the word. Send the message to me and tell me that you've read this book *Prophetic Evangelism Made Simple,* and you want feedback on your prophecy. I'll be delighted to give you constructive feedback on your prophecy and show you what gifts are in operation. I may even give you practice over some of my friends who will also give you feedback, if you want me to.

I pray that you'll go and prepare yourself. You may want to re-read the last chapter of the book if you like and then come back. Prepare yourself. Allow the presence of God to be active in your life. Believe

His anointing is flowing. (Satan will be trying desperately to block feelings!) Then open an e-mail to me or friend request me and send me a message and say, "Matthew, I feel the Lord wants to say to you today…" then type what comes.

thirty-four

Practice Makes Perfect

With anything in life, the more you practice a certain skill, the better you become. The gift of prophecy is a perfect gift. It says in James, "All good and perfect gifts come down from the Father of lights." And I have to agree that even the hundreds of people that have prophesied over me with their first prophecy, these prophecies have been meaningful and good. It's been a wonderful gift that people have received, so I always look forward to first prophecies by people. They really touch me and they bless me.

Some things improve with time, like a wine matures with age or a special sporting ability becomes better with practice, the more games you play. The same is true with prophecy: your gift actually sharpens and becomes better and you become more confident by giving words regularly. Your gift will mature. I encourage you to practice on people, to ask the Lord daily that He would give you opportunities to prophesy to a lot of people, and to go up and tap people on the shoulder and say, "Excuse me. I have a gift, and from time to time that gift allows me to receive a message for a person. Today I've received a message just for you."

Then launch into the prophecy. Tell them that God told you to give them the prophecy, watch them give you feedback, watch them say thank you. Then, go off and be available to the Lord so you can do the next one and the next one. Remember, people at church will be open to receive a prophetic word from you and they'll give you instant feedback. The Holy Spirit is in charge, so no one can be discouraged by what you have to say.

Therefore, take plenty of opportunities to prophesy over people at church. Of course, receive your pastor's permission first. If you feel you have a prophetic message for the whole church, it is absolutely essential to first run it by the Pastor. There may be a very good reason why he considers it to be unwise. Always trust in his leadership ability because he is answerable to God.

As you increase giving prophetic words to people, your ability strengthens and the hearer is edified. Scripture says that the gift of Prophecy is to be used to build up the body of Christ. Therefore, the Holy Spirit will give you words that are edifying to the hearer.

As your confidence strengthens, start to prophesy to strangers as the Lord highlights them for you. My name is Matthew Robert Payne, as you can see on the book cover and on my YouTube address.

I encourage you to contact me on Facebook under Matthew Robert Payne at this link.

http://www.facebook.com/people/Matthew-Robert-Payne/585589458

I encourage you to write to me at my e-mail address at this link. survivors.sanctuary@gmail.com

I encourage you to go online and check out my website and check out my books and contact me through my website at this link. http://www.matthewrobertpayneministries.net

Another great resource where you can learn to prophesy and practice is Inside Out Training and Equipping School on Facebook. They are very encouraging groups and it's a free service.

May God bless you abundantly! I encourage you to share this book with others, or share the link for this book on Amazon with your friends and family. Remember, if you want some of your friends to come with you and evangelize through the prophetic, it would be good to share this book with them. May God bless you and keep you in peace.

If you were helped by this book and were encouraged by it, could you please take five minutes and write a short review of the book on Amazon for me. The more positive reviews on Amazon, the more people will become equipped to prophesy in the streets of their city.

Made in the USA
Lexington, KY
09 February 2018